MODERN

Compiled by
Susanne Woods

BLOCKS

99 Quilt Blocks from Your Favorite Designers

Text, Photography, and Artwork copyright © 2011 by C&T Publishing, Inc.

Publisher: Amy Marson	Book Designer: April Mostek
Creative Director: Gailen Runge	Production Coordinator: Zinnia Heinzmann
Acquisitions Editor: Susanne Woods	Production Editor: Alice Mace Nakanishi
Editors: Lynn Koolish and Liz Aneloski	Illustrator: Mary E. Flynn
Technical Editors: Ann Haley and Gailen Runge	Photography by Christina Carty-Francis and Diane Pedersen of C&T Publishing, Inc., unless otherwise noted
Cover Designer: Kristy Zacharias	

Published by Stash Books, an imprint of C&T Publishing, Inc., P.O. Box 1456, Lafayette, CA 94549

Library of Congress Cataloging-in-Publication Data

Modern blocks : 99 quilt blocks from your favorite designers / compiled by Susanne Woods.
    p. cm.
 Summary: "The new kids on the block! Today's most talented modern quilters put a fresh and fun spin on 99 traditional block designs. Chock full of step-by-step instructions, how-to photographs and helpful hints, this collection of inspiring projects makes it easy for any sewer-no matter what level of expertise-to quilt in a modern style with impressive results"-- Provided by publisher.
 ISBN 978-1-60705-445-0 (soft cover)
 1. Patchwork quilts. 2. Quilting--Patterns. 3. Square in art. I. Woods, Susanne.
 TT835.M595 2011
 746.46--dc22
                              2011007726

Printed in China

10 9 8 7 6 5 4 3 2 1

CONTENTS

Introduction **7**

INTRODUCTION

I just love quilt blocks. They are so versatile and chameleon-like that they can totally change character with a simple change of colors or values. I love that they can stand alone as mini-quilts in their own right or be repeated in a multitude of settings to create infinite possibilities. Combine that with my love of modern quilting, and you begin to see why I wanted to compile this book!

In this book, you will find a collection of fabulous blocks from some of the most innovative designers. From gnomes and robots to clean lines and bold colors, these quilt blocks are distinctly modern. You won't find a Bow Tie block in the bunch, but you will find great textures, fresh color combinations, and unique creations. Some blocks use traditional piecing, some feature appliqué, and others are embellished with simple embroidery.

With the 12-inch block size, you can make a pillow from one of your favorite blocks or combine a few to create a uniquely modern quilt design of your own. Enlarge or reduce the designs for more variations. Our designers have also included their advice for larger quilt design possibilities and tips and tricks that they learned through their block construction.

So whether the chocolate ran into the peanut butter or the other way around, I hope you find these original blocks and the modern quilt movement just as irresistible a combination as the peanut butter cup (yum!). I can't wait to see what you make!

~Susanne Woods

HOW TO USE THIS BOOK

All of the blocks in *Modern Blocks* are designed to be 12½″ × 12½″ once they are constructed and 12″ × 12″ after they are sewn into a quilt. The only exception is the Arrowhead block on page 18, which was so fun we had to include it. All the other blocks can be mixed and matched to your heart's delight.

Another helpful feature of *Modern Blocks* is that all the block photos are 6″ × 6″, or exactly 50% of what the finished block will be if you follow the instructions given.

Pick one block and follow the designer's suggestions to lay out an entire quilt or make a modern sampler using all your favorites.

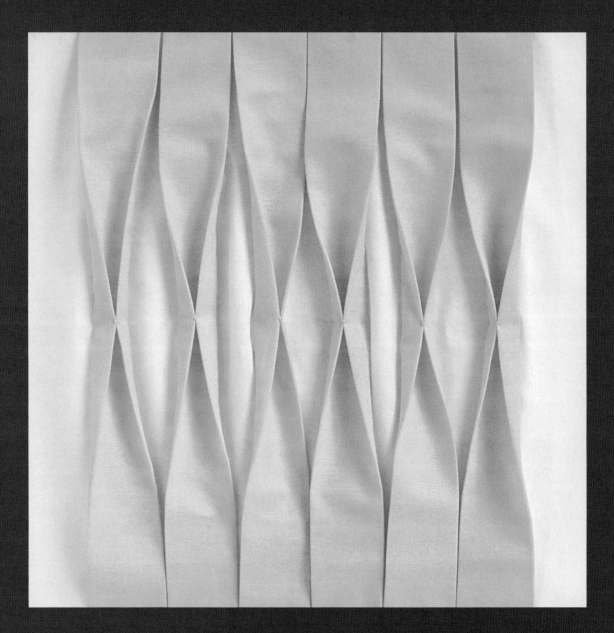

designed by Ellen Luckett Baker

A TWIST OF **LEMON**

This pleated quilt block will add texture and style to any project.
It's easier than it looks. Most of the work is done by folding and
pressing the box pleats.

SUPPLIES AND CUTTING

Yellow fabric for pleats

Cut 6 strips 3½" × 12½".

White fabric for background

Cut 2 strips 2¾" × 12½".

Cut 5 strips 2" × 12½".

Fabric marker

HOW-TO

Use ¼" seam allowances.

1. With right sides together, sew the strips together, alternating 6 yellow 3½" × 12½" pleat strips with 5 white 2" × 12½" background strips. Add the white 2¾" × 12½" background strips to the right and left sides of the alternating strips as shown. Press the seams to one side.

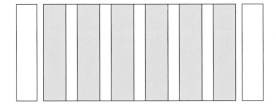

2. On the wrong side, mark the top and bottom centers of each yellow fabric section with a fabric marker. Working from the back of the piece and starting at one end, bring the first background strip to the center marks, so the seam meets the center marks. Pin and press. Repeat with the next background strip, so the 2 seams meet at the center marks on the wrong side of the yellow fabric strip, forming a box pleat on the front of the fabric. Repeat to form 5 box pleats.

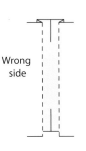

Wrong side

3. Machine baste ⅛" from the edge along the top and bottom of the block to hold the pleats in place.

4. On the right side of each yellow box pleat, find the center and pinch the folded edges together as shown in the block photo (page 8). Hand stitch each pinched pleat in place with a small tack stitch in matching thread.

AFTER **HOURS** designed by Louise Papas

This block is a simple needle-turn appliqué project and should be done in a free-form way. Make yourself an entire city skyline with a row of blocks or keep it fairly simple with just a few.

SUPPLIES AND CUTTING

Note: Cutting measurements include ¼″ seam allowances.

Light gray fabric for background

Cut 1 square 13½″ × 13½″. Trim to 12½″ × 12½″ after appliqué.

Dark gray fabric for tall building

Cut 1 rectangle 4½″ × 9″.

Medium gray fabric for smaller buildings

Cut 1 rectangle 3″ × 6″ for the left building. Cut 1 rectangle 3″ × 7½″ for the building on the right.

Yellow fabric for windows

Cut 11 rectangles varying in size from 1½″ × 2½″ for the large windows to 1¼″ × 1¾″ for the narrow windows.

HOW-TO

1. Fold the background fabric in half in both directions and finger-press to find the center point. Center the dark gray rectangle from right to left on the background fabric, with the lower edge approximately 2″ from the bottom of the square. Pin in place and appliqué using a needle-turn technique.

2. Using the project photo (page 10) as a guide, pin the medium gray buildings on either side of the tall building, making sure the buildings line up at the bottom and butt up against each other.

3. Appliqué the windows onto each building.

4. Trim the block to 12½″ × 12½″.

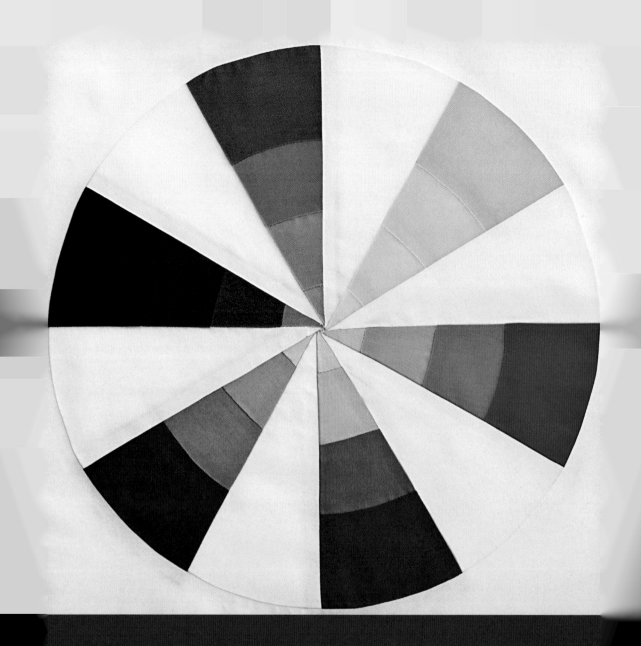

ALL OR **NOTHING** designed by Angela Ping

This block uses a pieced circle technique that may require
some practice. Challenging? Maybe, but worth it.

SUPPLIES AND CUTTING

Template patterns are on page 207.

½ yard white fabric

Cut 1 square 15″ × 15″ for the block background. Trim the block to 12½″ × 12½″ after assembly.

Cut 6 wedges from Template A.

4 shades each of red, orange, yellow, green, blue, and purple fabrics

For each color group, cut 4 rectangles 4″ × 6″, ranging from light to dark.

From each of the 6 color groupings, cut 1 each using Templates B, C, D, and E.

TIP For each color group, use Template B for the lightest fabric, Template C for the light/medium fabric, Template D for the medium/dark fabric, and Template E for the darkest fabric.

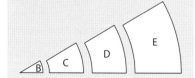

HOW-TO

Use ¼″ seam allowances.

1. With right sides together, sew the B, C, D and E wedges of color together with curved seams. Press the seam allowances toward the outside of the circle.

2. With right sides together, sew the color wedges to the white wedges in pairs. Sew accurately, marking the point where the ¼″ seam allowances overlap; stop sewing at that point and backstitch. Sew from the outer edge toward the center.

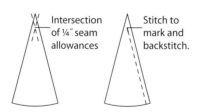

Intersection of ¼″ seam allowances

Stitch to mark and backstitch.

3. With right sides together, sew the wedge pairs together to make 2 half-circles; then sew the half-circles together. Press the seams in one direction.

4. Fold the background square in half in both directions. Draw a quarter-circle with a radius of 5½″. Cut along the drawn line and remove the inner circle.

Fold

Fold

5½″

5. On the background square, stay-stitch ⅛″ away from the cut circle.

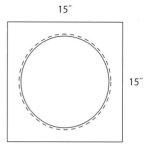

15″

15″

6. Make 12 pencil marks around the cut-out circle in equal increments of 30°. Place the pieced circle, right side up, on top of the background fabric, also right side up, matching the seamlines to the marks around the circle.

7. Flip over the background fabric at each marked point so it is right sides together with the center pieced circle. Pin thoroughly.

8. Stitch the circle to the background. Press the seam toward the background fabric. Clip the outer curve if needed. Trim the block to 12½″ × 12½″.

ALLEYWAYS
designed by
Weeks Ringle and Bill Kerr

This block sets four smaller, improvised units within a grid.
When multiple blocks are combined, unexpected juxtapositions of color
bring new delight, surprising even you, the maker.

SUPPLIES AND CUTTING

Assorted fabrics

Cut 16–20 strips 7″ long and approximately 1½″ wide at one end and 2¼″ wide at the other.

Off-white fabric

Cut 2 strips 1½″ × 6″.

Cut 1 strip 1½″ × 12½″.

HOW-TO

Use ¼″ seam allowances.

1. With right sides together, sew 4 or 5 strips together to form a piece that is larger than 6½″ × 6½″. Press the seams open.

2. Trim the piece to 6″ × 6″.

3. Repeat Steps 1 and 2 to make 4 squares 6″ × 6″.

4. With right sides together, sew a 6″ × 6″ square to each long side of a 1½″ × 6″ off-white strip. Press the seams open. Repeat with the 2 remaining 6″ × 6″ squares and the other 1½″ × 6″ off-white strip. Press the seams open.

5. Sew a 1½″ × 12½″ off-white strip between the 2 units created in Step 4 to complete the block.

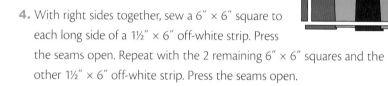

APRIL **SHOWERS** designed by Kirsti Underwood

Perfect for both novice and advanced stitchers,
this sweet, simple pattern uses just two kinds of stitches—
backstitch and French knots—and is easy to complete quickly.

SUPPLIES AND CUTTING

Muslin

Cut 1 square 15½" × 15½". Trim to
12½" × 12½" after embroidery.

**6-strand embroidery floss or perle
cotton thread in various colors**

Pencil or iron-on transfer pen

HOW-TO

1. Trace the pattern from the block photo (page 16) and enlarge the drawing
by 200%.

2. Tape the enlarged pattern onto a bright window. Center the fabric (or
paper if you are using a transfer pen) over the pattern and tape it in place.
Trace the design using a pencil or iron-on transfer pen (follow the manufacturer's instructions).

3. Stitch the pattern. Work all of the backstitch first; then work the French
knots. Use 6 strands of floss for everything except the mouths of the
clouds and flowers—for those, use 2 strands. The eyes of the clouds and
flowers are French knots that use 6 strands of floss wrapped twice around
the needle.

4. Trim the block to 12½" × 12½".

ARROWHEAD designed by Wendy Hill

I adapted a mathematical triangle pattern
found all around the world in architecture, tiles, and painted designs.
A shortcut makes the block construction easy.

SUPPLIES AND CUTTING

3 contrasting fabrics

Cut 1 rectangle 3″ × 6½″ and 1 rectangle 2¼″ × 2¾″ from each fabric.

HOW-TO

Use ¼″ seam allowances. The template pattern is on page 207.

1. Use the pattern (page 207) to make a template for the triangle shape. Punch a small hole in the template where indicated on the pattern.

2. Trace around the template on the *wrong side* of each 3″ × 6½″ rectangle and mark the seam intersection at the hole in the template with a pencil.

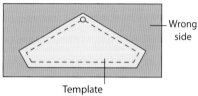

Wrong side

Template

3. With right sides together, piece the 3 triangle shapes together with a Y-seam as shown. Always sew from the outside edge to the middle, stopping and backstitching at the marked point.

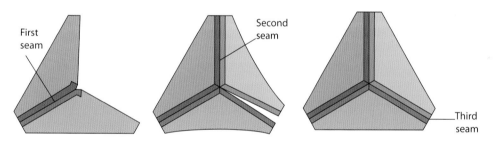

First seam

Second seam

Third seam

4. Press the seams open.

5. With right sides together, center the long edge of a 2¼″ × 2¾″ rectangle with a triangle point. Sew the seam, backstitching at the start and finish of the seamline. Press open. Repeat with the remaining 2 small rectangles.

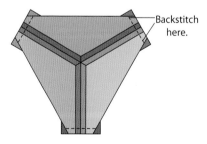

Backstitch here.

6. Trim the rectangles to create a triangle.

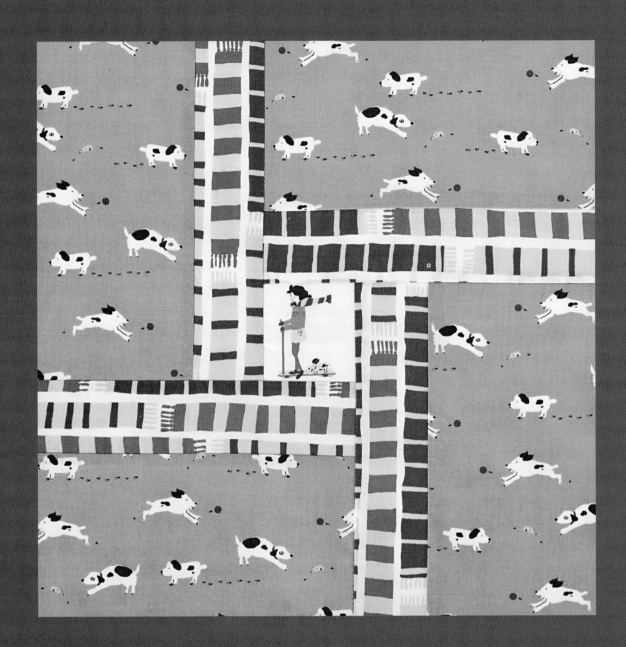

BEST **FRIEND** designed by Angela Pingel

This block is perfect for medium- and large-scale prints that are difficult to cut for fear of losing the design. If the focal fabric is directional, think about cutting it so that the print all runs the same way. Or create movement by cutting the fabric so the pattern changes direction with each piece. This is the perfect block to use with layer cakes or fat quarter bundles of a collection!

SUPPLIES AND CUTTING

White print fabric

Cut 1 square 2½″ × 2½″ (A).

Stripe fabric

Cut 4 strips 2″ × 7½″ (B).

Print fabric

Cut 4 rectangles 4″ × 7½″ (C).
You may want to cut these
directionally.

HOW-TO

Use ¼″ seam allowances.

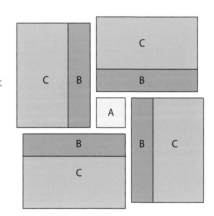

1. Arrange the pieces, using the block
photo (page 20) as a guide.

2. With right sides together, sew
each B to a C. If you are using
directional fabrics for C, be sure to
pay attention to which pieces are
sewn together.

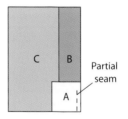

3. With right sides together, sew the center square
to the lower right edge of a B/C segment, starting
midway with a backstitch to make a partial seam.

4. Sew the remaining B/C segments around the
center square A in a counterclockwise direction.
Press all the seams away from the center square.

5. Complete the partial seam between the first B/C segment and the center
square A.

6. Trim the block to 12½″ × 12½″.

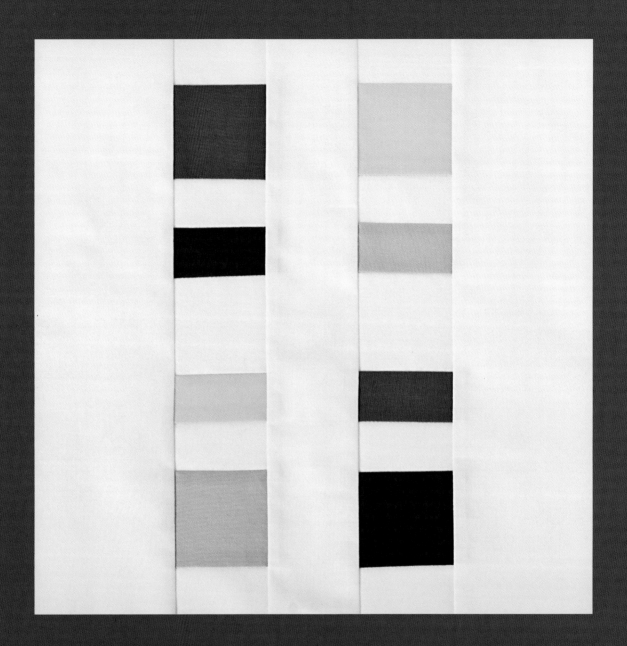

BINARY designed by Angela Pingel

There are many ways to use this design. For a twist, change the arrangement
of colors in each block. Alternatively, keep the white background consistent and use
different colors in each block. Also, try rotating the block 90 degrees
to change the look from block to block in a quilt.

SUPPLIES AND CUTTING

¼ yard white fabric

    Cut 2 strips 3½" × 12½".

    Cut 1 strip 2½" × 12½".

    Cut 8 strips 2½" × 1½".

    Cut 2 squares 2½" × 2½".

3" × 5" each yellow, gray, light gray, and purple fabrics

    Cut 1 rectangle 1½" × 2½" and 1 square 2½" × 2½" from each color.

HOW-TO

Use ¼" seam allowances.

1. Using the block photo (page 22) as a guide, arrange the 1½" × 2½" white and colored rectangles and the 2½" × 2½" white and colored squares into 2 columns.

2. With right sides together, sew the colored pieces to the white pieces along the 2½" edges to create 2 columns 2½" × 12½".

3. With right sides together, sew a pieced column to either side of the 2½" × 12½" white strip. Press the seams away from the pieced columns.

4. Add a 3½" × 12½" white strip to either side of the unit from Step 3. Press the seams away from the pieced columns.

5. Trim the block to 12½" × 12½".

BIRDSONG
designed by
Rachel Roxburgh

Although not a traditional block, Birdsong is deceptively easy to make. It is a simple combination of squares, rectangles, appliqué, and a little embroidery.

SUPPLIES AND CUTTING

Trace the appliqué and embroidery designs from the block photo (page 24) and enlarge by 200%.

Fabric A (linen)

Cut 1 rectangle 7″ × 8″.

Fabrics B, C, D, and E

Cut 1 square 3″ × 3″ from each fabric.

Fabrics F and H

Cut 1 rectangle 1½″ × 8″ from each fabric.

Fabric G

Cut 1 rectangle 2½″ × 10½″.

Fabric I

Cut 1 rectangle 2″ × 8″.

Fabric J

Cut 1 rectangle 2½″ × 12½″.

Fabric scraps for appliqué

Cut 5 flower petals and 2 leaves; add seam allowances for turned-under appliqué.

Cut a 3″ × 4″ rectangle for the bird.

Cut 1 circle 3″ in diameter to make a yo-yo for the flower center.

5″ green rickrack

Paper-backed fusible web

Perle cotton thread in brown, pink, and green

HOW-TO

Use ¼″ seam allowances.

1. With right sides together and pressing each seam as you go, sew pieces in this order:

   - A to F
   - B to C
   - D to E
   - B/C to D/E
   - H to I
   - H/I to A/F
   - B/C/D/E to H/I/A/F
   - G to right side
   - J to top

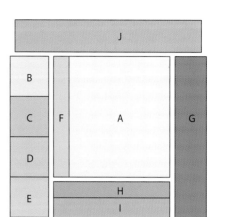

2. Reverse the bird pattern and trace it on the paper side of the fusible web. Iron the fusible web to the wrong side of the bird fabric (following the manufacturer's instructions). Cut out the bird and fuse it in place on the block. Topstitch around the edge of the bird.

3. Machine stitch the rickrack stem in place.

4. Pin the petals and leaves in place. Hand appliqué, turning under the seam allowance as you go.

5. Make a yo-yo by stitching a running stitch around the edge of the 3″ circle and pulling it until the opening closes. Take a few stitches to hold it firmly closed. Stitch the yo-yo to the center of the flower with the gathered side facing up.

6. Transfer the embroidery design onto the block either freehand or by putting the pattern underneath your block on a light table or in a bright window and tracing. Embroider the butterfly, bird, petal, and leaf details with running stitches and backstitches.

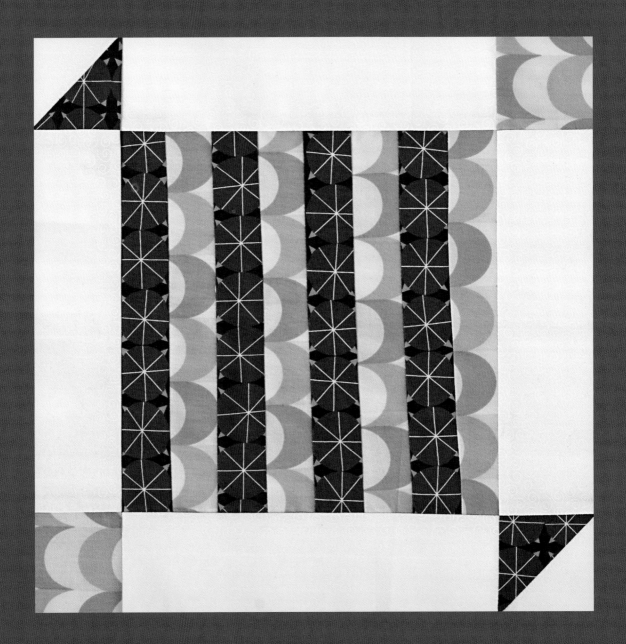

BLUE **LAGOON** designed by Pat Sloan

A spin on a more traditional block, this block is awesome set side by side
or alternated with another type of block.

SUPPLIES AND CUTTING

White fabric

Cut 4 strips 2½″ × 8½″.

Cut 1 square 2⅞″ × 2⅞″.

Light blue fabric

Cut 2 squares 2½″ × 2½″.

Cut 4 strips 1½″ × 8½″.

Dark blue fabric

Cut 1 square 2⅞″ × 2⅞″.

Cut 4 strips 1½″ × 8½″.

HOW-TO

Use ¼″ seam allowances.

1. Use the 2⅞″ × 2⅞″ squares of white and dark blue to make 2 half-square triangle units (see instructions, at right).

2. With right sides together, sew the light and dark blue 1½″ × 8½″ strips together, alternating light and dark blue for the center of the block. Press.

3. With right sides together, sew a 2½″ × 8½″ white strip to either side of the blue center unit. Press.

4. With right sides together, sew a light blue square to one end of a 2½″ × 8½″ white strip and a half-square triangle unit to the other end, using the illustration in Step 5 for guidance. Make 2. Press.

5. With right sides together, sew the units from Step 4 to the top and bottom of the center unit to complete the block. Press.

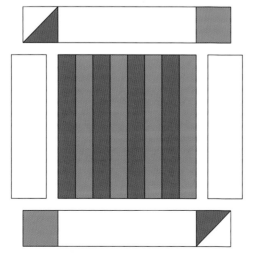

HALF-SQUARE TRIANGLE UNITS

Refer to the project instructions for the size of the squares.

1. With right sides together, pair 2 squares. Lightly draw a diagonal line from one corner to the opposite corner on the wrong side of a square.

Draw line.

2. Sew a ¼″ seam on each side of the line.

Sew.

3. Cut on the drawn line.

4. Press and trim off the dog-ears.

HALF-SQUARE TRIANGLE UNITS

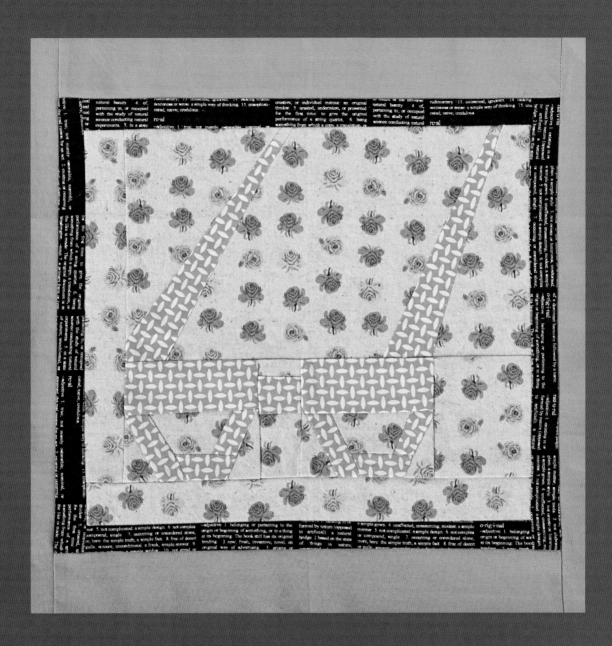

BLUE **SPECS**

designed by
Penny Michelle Layman

The center of this block is foundation pieced and then background
strips are added to the left and bottom. It is then framed with black
newsprint strips and taupe linen for a chic finish.

SUPPLIES AND CUTTING

¼ yard or fat quarter (18″ × 22″) print fabric for background

Cut 1 strip 1½″ × 8½″.

Cut 1 strip 1½″ × 10½″.

Use the remaining fabric for foundation piecing.

⅛ yard blue fabric for specs

Newsprint fabric for inner border

Cut 4 strips 1½″ × 10½″.

Tan fabric for outer border

Cut 2 strips 1¼″ × 11½″ for the top and bottom outer borders.

Cut 2 strips 1¼″ × 12½″ for the side outer borders.

Foundation paper, such as Simple Foundations Translucent Vellum Paper or Carol Doak's Foundation Paper

HOW-TO

Use ¼″ seam allowances.

TIP If you are not familiar with paper piecing, try one of the following resources (by C&T Publishing).

· *Every Quilter's Foundation Piecing Reference Tool* by Jane Hall and Dixie Haywood

· *Carol Doak Teaches You to Paper Piece* DVD

LENSES

Enlarge the foundation patterns (page 208) by 200%.

1. Foundation piece one of the lens units, adding the pieces in numerical order. Make certain the outer pieces extend at least ¼″ beyond all sides of the lens unit. Trim the seam allowance to ¼″ on all sides of the lens unit. Make 2.

2. Piece the bridge unit in numerical order, leaving a ¼″ seam allowance on all sides.

3. With right sides together, sew the bridge unit between the lens units. Do not remove the paper until the entire block is complete.

4. Add a 2½″ × 3½″ background rectangle to the right side of the unit from Step 3.

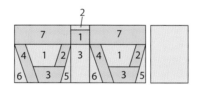

Lenses

TEMPLES

1. Foundation piece each temple of the spectacles; then add the background fabric to complete the temple unit. Trim the seam allowance to ¼″ on all sides of the temple unit. Press.

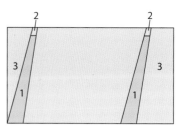

Temples

2. With right sides together, sew the temple unit to the lenses unit and trim to 9½″ × 8½″.

BLOCK ASSEMBLY

1. Add a 1½″ × 8½″ background strip to the left side of the foundation-pieced unit. Press.

2. Add a 1½″ × 10½″ background strip to the bottom of the foundation-pieced unit. Press. Trim to 10½″ × 9½″.

BORDERS

1. Sew 1″ × 10½″ newsprint inner border strips to the top and bottom of the block and press.

2. Sew 1″ × 10½″ newsprint inner border strips to the left and right sides of the block and press.

3. For the outer border, sew 1¼″ × 11½″ tan strips to the top and bottom of the block and press.

4. Sew 1¼″ × 12½″ tan strips to the left and right sides of the block.

5. Press and trim the block to 12½″ × 12½″. Remove the foundation paper.

BOTANICAL

designed by
Louise Papas

With its various shades of green, this block will suit those who like more natural, earthy tones and themes. Designed for hand sewing, this is a lovely needle-turn appliqué project that can also easily be blanket stitched by hand or raw-edge appliquéd using a sewing machine if preferred.

SUPPLIES AND CUTTING

To make the patterns, trace the design from the block photo (page 30) and enlarge the drawing by 200%.

Tan fabric for background

Cut 1 square 13½″ × 13½″. Trim to 12½″ × 12½″ after appliqué.

12″ × 12″ green solid fabric

Cut 1 large leaf shape.*

7 squares 3″ × 3″ green fabric

Cut 1 leaf marking A.*

Cut 4 leaf markings B.*

Cut 2 leaf markings C.*

* Use your favorite appliqué method. Add a ¼″ seam allowance when cutting shapes if you are using a needle-turn appliqué method.

HOW-TO

1. Fold the background fabric in half in both directions and finger-press to find the center point.

2. Position, pin, and appliqué the leaf.

3. Position, pin, and appliqué the inner shapes.

4. Trim the block to 12½″ × 12½″.

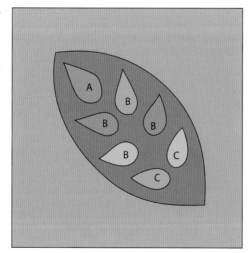

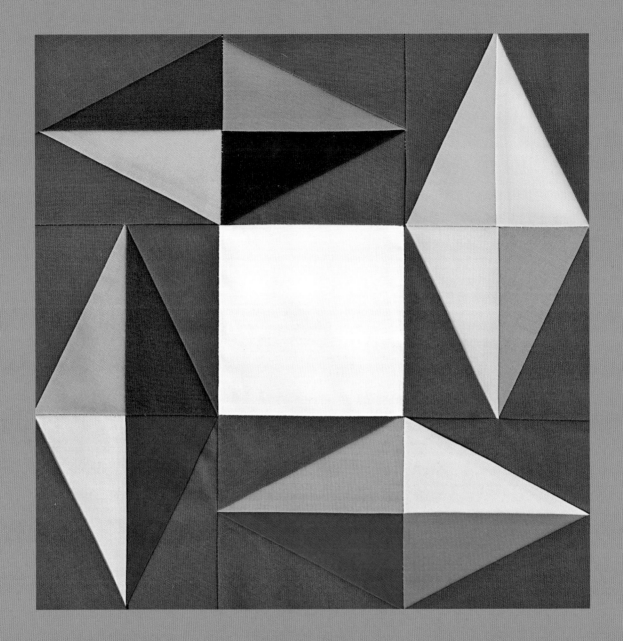

BOX **KITE** designed by
Angela Pingel

With the right placement of color and light, these diamonds appear almost three-dimensional. Use high contrast for adjacent pieces of the diamond and lower contrast for pieces diagonally across from one another. A neutral background and center allow the diamonds to sparkle.

SUPPLIES AND CUTTING

The template pattern is on page 207.

¼ yard gray fabric

Cut 8 triangles using Template A.

Cut 8 triangles using Template A reversed.

White fabric

Cut 1 square 4½" × 4½" for the center.

16 fabric scraps 4" × 6" (2 dark shades and 2 light shades each of orange, yellow, blue, and purple)

Cut 8 triangles (2 dark shades of each color) using Template A.

Cut 8 triangles (2 light shades of each color) using Template A reversed.

HOW-TO

Use ¼" seam allowances.

1. Arrange the pieces, using the block photo (page 32) as a guide.

2. With right sides together, sew a gray triangle A to each dark triangle A along the long edges. Press the seams open.

3. With right sides together, sew a gray reverse triangle A to a light colored reverse triangle A along the long edges. Press the seams open.

4. Sew the rectangles from Steps 2 and 3 into pairs as shown.

5. Arrange the square units from Step 4 around the 4½" × 4½" white square as shown. Carefully matching the seam intersections and aligning the points of the triangles, assemble the squares into rows.

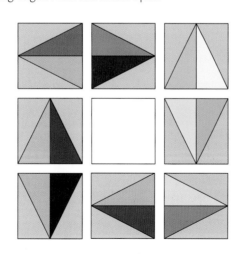

6. With right sides together, sew the rows together.

7. Trim the block to 12½" × 12½".

BOXED **IN**

designed by
Faith Jones

This block has four quadrants. The portion of each quadrant
that forms the center of the final block varies in size. Be creative
when you select fabrics. Consider incorporating a solid neutral fabric,
such as white, into each quadrant.

SUPPLIES AND CUTTING

Dark green fabric

Cut 1 square 2″ × 2″ (A).

Light green fabric

Cut 1 strip 2″ × 5½″ (B).

Cut 1 rectangle 7″ × 5½″ (C).

Light pink fabric

Cut 1 square 4″ × 4″ (D).

Dark pink fabric

Cut 1 rectangle 3½″ × 4″ (E).

Cut 1 strip 7″ × 3½″ (F).

Light orange fabric

Cut 1 square 3″ × 3″ (G).

Dark orange fabric

Cut 1 rectangle 4½″ × 3″ (H).

Cut 1 rectangle 7 × 4½″ (I).

Light blue fabric

Cut 1 square 5″ × 5″ (J).

Dark blue fabric

Cut 1 strip 2½″ × 5″ (K).

Cut 1 strip 7″ × 2½″ (L).

HOW-TO

Use ¼″ seam allowances.

1. With right sides together, sew each quadrant as diagrammed. Refer to the block photo (page 34) as needed.

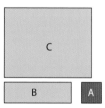

Upper left quadrant

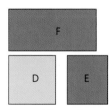

Upper right quadrant

Lower left quadrant

Lower right quadrant

2. Sew the quadrants together.

3. Trim the block to 12½″ × 12½″.

BOXED **UP** designed by Angela Yosten

This block was inspired by nested boxes that stack within each other. When put together into a quilt, this block results in a great geometric look—great for the boys (or men) in your life.

SUPPLIES AND CUTTING

Gray fabric 1

Cut 1 square 4½″ × 4½″ (A).

Green fabric

Cut 1 square 4½″ × 4½″ (B).

Cut 1 strip 8½″ × 4½″ (C).

Gray fabric 2

Cut 1 strip 4½″ × 8½″ (D).

Cut 1 strip 12½″ × 4½″ (E).

HOW-TO

Use ¼″ seam allowances.

1. With right sides together, sew the 4½″ × 4½″ gray square A to the 4½″ × 4½″ green square B. Press toward the green square.

2. With right sides together, sew the green 8½″ × 4½″ strip C to the top of the squares from Step 1. Press toward the green fabric.

3. With right sides together, sew the 4½″ × 8½″ gray strip D to the left side of the unit from Step 2. Press toward the gray fabric.

4. With right sides together, sew the 12½″ × 4½″ gray strip E to the top of the unit from Step 3. Press toward the gray fabric.

5. Trim the block to 12½″ × 12½″.

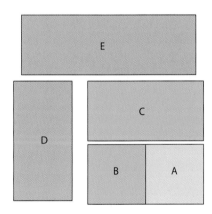

designed by Angela Yosten

CHECKERED **FIELDS**

This graphic block is great for showcasing a favorite color or fabric.
Although its simple pattern and straightforward construction require
precision when sewing, it is a good block for beginners.

SUPPLIES AND CUTTING

Medium blue tone-on-tone fabric

   Cut 2 strips 1″ × 6″.

   Cut 2 strips 1″ × 6½″.

Light green tone-on-tone fabric

   Cut 2 squares 6″ × 6″.

Medium green tone-on-tone fabric

   Cut 2 squares 6½″ × 6½″.

Spray starch (*optional*)

> **TIP** Lightly spray the medium blue fabric with starch to help the narrow strips hold their shape during block construction.

HOW-TO

Use ¼″ seam allowances.

1. With right sides together, sew a 1″ × 6″ medium blue strip to each light green square. If you are using a directional fabric, you will need to sew the 1″ × 6″ medium blue strip to the right side of a light green square (A) and to the left side of the other square (B), so that the image appears upright in the finished block. Press.

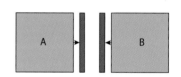

2. With right sides together, sew a 1″ × 6½″ medium blue strip to the bottom of a light green square A and to the top of the other square B. Press. Label the blocks A and B.

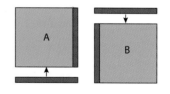

3. With right sides together, sew a medium green square to the right side of pieced square A. Sew the other medium green square to the left side of pieced square B. Press.

4. With right sides together, sew the top set of squares to the bottom set, matching the center seams. Press.

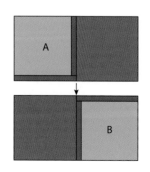

CHECKERS designed by
Monika Wintermantel

This is a great block for a bee group—each member can add her own fabrics
and show her creativity by adding an appliqué.

SUPPLIES AND CUTTING

Assorted print fabrics

Cut 20 squares 2″ × 2″ for the inner border.

Cut 16 squares 1¼″ × 1¼″ for the outer corner squares.

White fabric

Cut 1 square 6½″ × 6½″ for the appliqué background.

Tan fabric

Cut 4 strips 2″ × 9½″ for the outer border.

Fabric scraps for appliqué

Paper-backed fusible web

HOW-TO

APPLIQUÉ

1. Trace the appliqué pieces from the block photo (page 40) and enlarge the drawing by 200%.

2. Reverse the shapes and trace them onto the paper side of the fusible web. Cut out the shapes ¼″ outside the drawn lines.

3. Iron the cut-out shapes of fusible web onto the wrong side of the appliqué fabric (following the manufacturer's instructions). Cut out the fabric pieces on the drawn lines and peel off the backing paper.

4. Arrange and fuse the fabric pieces onto the white square. Stitch around the shapes with black thread. Add a line of stitching for the dog to stand upon.

5. Draw or embroider the question mark, dog's eye, and wag marks near the tail.

BORDERS

Use ¼″ seam allowances.

1. With right sides together, sew 4 of the 2″ × 2″ squares into a row. Press the seams in one direction. Repeat to make 2 rows of 4 squares.

2. With right sides together, sew 6 of the 2″ × 2″ squares into a row. Press the seams in one direction. Repeat to make 2 rows of 6 squares.

3. With right sides together, sew the 4-square rows to the top and bottom of the center square. Sew the 6-square rows to the sides of the center square. Press toward the pieced rows.

4. With right sides together, sew the 1¼″ × 1¼″ squares together to make 4 four-patch units.

5. Sew 2″ × 9½″ tan strips to the left and right sides of the block. Press.

6. Sew a four-patch unit from Step 4 to each end of the 2 remaining 2″ × 9½″ tan strips. Sew these assembled strips to the top and bottom of the block. Press.

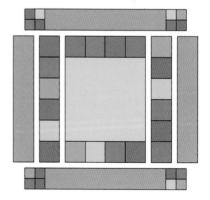

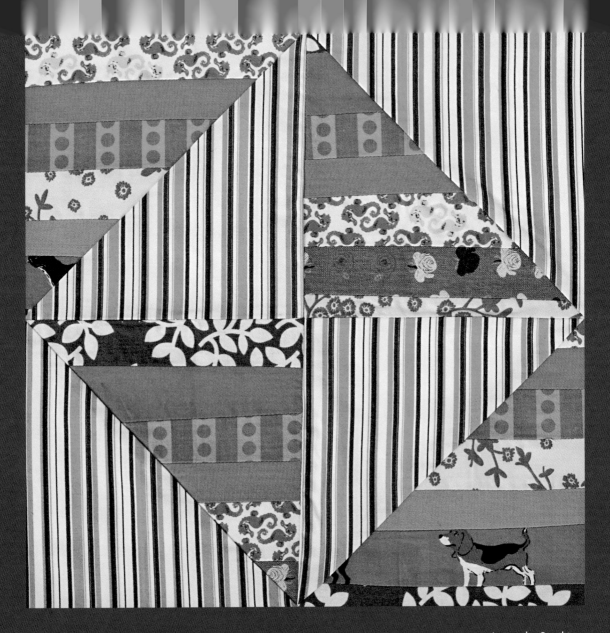

designed by Amanda Sasikirana

CRISS-CROSS **TRIANGLES**

You will need small amounts of multiple fabrics to make this block,

so it is an excellent way to use up scraps.

SUPPLIES AND CUTTING

Striped fabric

Cut 2 squares 6⅞" × 6⅞".

Accent fabrics

Cut 16 strips 1½"* × 7½".

*Vary the width of the strips from 1" to
2" for greater interest.*

HOW-TO

Use ¼" seam allowances.

1. With right sides together, sew the
accent strips together along the
7½" edges to create a rectangle at
least 16" × 7½". Press the seam
allowances to one side.

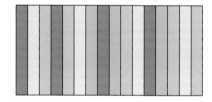

2. Cut 2 squares 6⅞" × 6⅞" from the accent fabric rectangle created
in Step 1.

3. With right sides together, sew a striped fabric square to an accent fabric
square to yield 2 half-square triangle units (page 27). Make sure the stripes
on both squares are going in the same direction. Repeat with the other
squares.

4. With right sides together, sew the
half-square triangles together in pairs as
shown. Press. Join the pairs together to form
a Four-Patch block. Press.

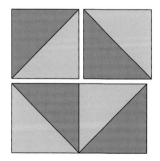

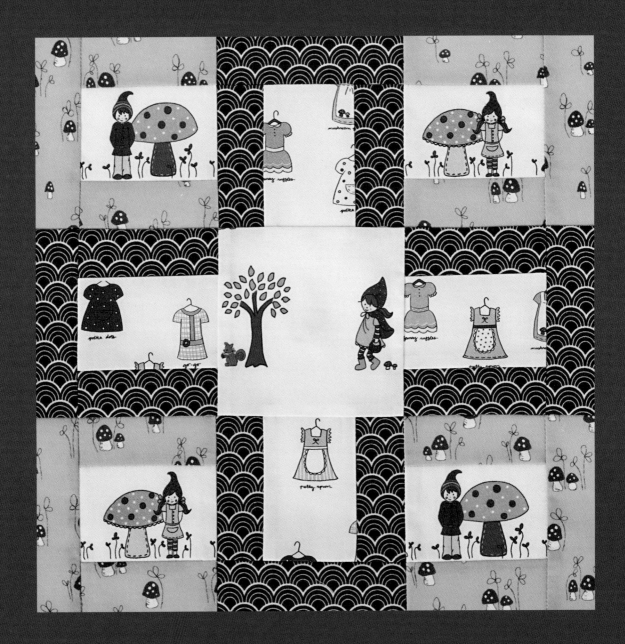

CROSSWALK designed by Angela Pingel

Though you may not see it at first, this block acts like a Nine-Patch block, showcasing a special fussy-cut fabric in the center. Use the rest of the block to help focus on the center. Sew as accurately as possible, using a ¼″ seam allowance to help maintain the correct dimensions.

SUPPLIES AND CUTTING

Fussy-cut fabric for centers

Cut 1 square 4½" × 4½"
for the center (D).

Cut 8 rectangles 2½" × 3½" (C).*

Red fabric**

Cut 4 strips 1½" × 4½" (A).

Cut 8 strips 1½" × 3½" (B).

Blue fabric**

Cut 4 strips 1½" × 4½" (A).

Cut 8 strips 1½" × 3½" (B).

* The rectangles for the patches above and below the center square should be fussy cut with a vertical orientation. The other six rectangles should be fussy cut as horizontal rectangles.

** These strips were fussy cut as well. Watch for directionality in your fabric and cut accordingly.

HOW-TO

Use ¼" seam allowances.

1. Lay out the cut pieces as shown.

2. Construct each of the 8 units surrounding the center square by sewing a B strip to either side of a fussy-cut C rectangle. Press. Sew an A strip to the outer end of each B/C/B unit. Press.

3. Sew the 3 units in Row 1 together and press their seams in one direction.

4. Sew the 3 units in Row 2 together and press their seams in the opposite direction from Row 1.

5. Sew the 3 units in Row 3 together and press their seams in the opposite direction from Row 2.

6. With right sides together, sew Row 1 to Row 2 and then add Row 3.

7. Trim the block to 12½" × 12½".

designed by Lara Finlayson

DIAMOND **RIPPLES**

This block is made from 36 half-square triangle units. The fun is in arranging them into the off-center diamond; then it's a simple matter of sewing them together. There are lots of seams in this block, so sew accurately!

SUPPLIES AND CUTTING

16″ × 10″ solid fabric

Cut 18 squares 2⅞″ × 2⅞″.

6 print fabrics, 3½″ × 9½″ each

Cut 3 squares 2⅞″ × 2⅞″
from each print.

Pencil or Hera marker

HOW-TO

Use ¼″ seam allowances.

1. Lightly draw or score a diagonal line from one corner to the opposite
corner on the wrong side of each solid square.

2. With right sides together, pair a print square and a solid square. Sew a
¼″ seam on each side of the drawn line. (See Half-Square Triangle Units,
page 27, for more guidance.) Make 36 half-square triangle units.

3. Referring to the block photo (page 46), arrange the units in 6 rows
of 6 units 2½″ × 2½″.

4. With right sides together, sew the units into rows. Press the seams in
adjacent rows in opposite directions.

5. With right sides together, sew the rows together. Press.

DIAMOND RIPPLES

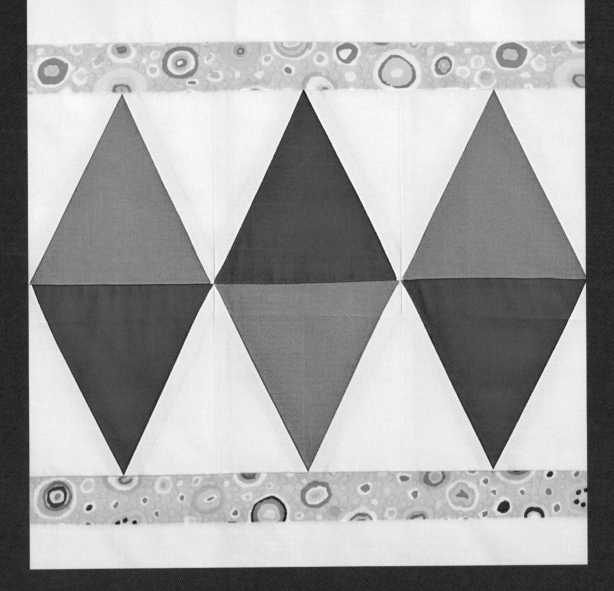

designed by Krista Hennebury

DIAMOND **TRIPTYCH**

This is a graphic, modern quilt block highlighting two solid colors in a diamond
shape reminiscent of a harlequin or argyle pattern. Choose a multicolored print
for the horizontal stripes; then choose colors from the print for the triangles.

SUPPLIES AND CUTTING

Template patterns are on page 208.

White fabric

Cut 2 strips 1½″ × 12½″.

Cut 6 triangles using Template A.

Cut 6 triangles using Template A reversed.

Green fabric

Cut 3 triangles using Template B.

Blue fabric

Cut 3 triangles using Template B.

Print fabric

Cut 2 strips 1½″ × 12½″.

Stiff template plastic

HOW-TO

Use ¼″ seam allowances.

1. With right sides together, sew a 1½″ × 12½″ white strip to a 1½″ × 12½″ print strip along the long edges. Press toward the print. Repeat with the remaining white and print strips.

2. With right sides together, match the angled (bias) edge of a blue triangle B to a white triangle A. Sew with a ¼″ seam allowance. Press toward the white background.

3. Repeat Step 2, adding a white reversed triangle A to the other side of the blue triangle B, creating a 4½″ × 4½″ square unit. Sew the remaining white background A's to the other blue and green triangles in the same fashion.

4. With right sides together, sew a blue/white unit from Step 3 to a green/white unit from Step 3 along the bases of the triangles. Press the seam open. Repeat with the remaining blue and green square units.

5. With right sides together, sew the rectangles from Step 4, alternating the triangle colors and carefully matching the center seams of the diamonds. Press the seams open to reduce bulk.

6. Attach the print and white strips from Step 1 to the top and bottom of the diamond row. Press toward the print. Trim the block to 12½″ × 12½″.

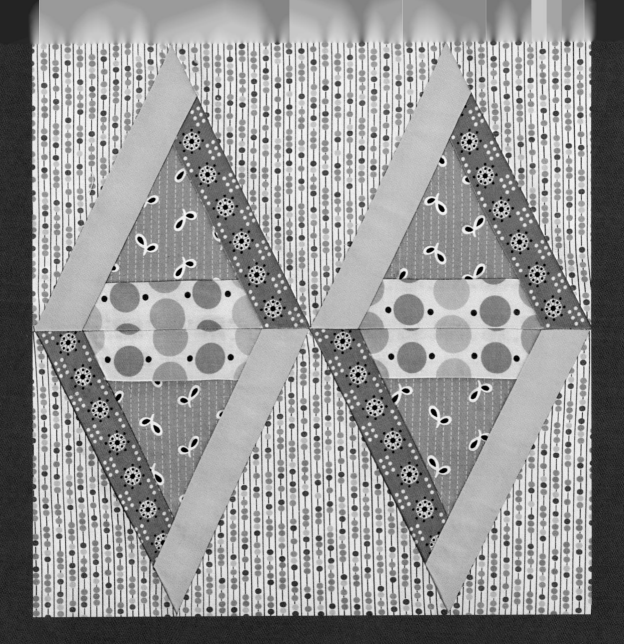

DOUBLEMINT
designed by
Angela Pingel

This block combines both paper piecing and templates to create a
one-of-a-kind design. The Log Cabin–style triangles are paper pieced
for accuracy, and the background fabric is cut from templates. The visual simplicity
of the block makes it perfect for quilts, whether all the blocks are done in the same
fabrics or varied, or whether they are kept in the same direction or rotated.

SUPPLIES AND CUTTING

Template and foundation patterns are on page 209.

1 fat quarter (18" × 22") background print fabric

Cut 2 using Template A.

Cut 2 using Template A reversed.

Cut 2 B triangles.*

* Use the outer edge (including seam allowances) of the pieced foundation template pattern (page 209) as a template pattern for the B triangles.

Blue print fabric

Cut 4 squares 4" × 4" for the centers of the pieced triangles.

Blue-and-white circle print fabric

Cut 1 strip 2" × width of fabric.

Dark green print fabric

Cut 1 strip 2" × width of fabric.

Light green solid fabric

Cut 1 strip 2" × width of fabric.

Foundation paper, such as Simple Foundations Translucent Vellum Paper or Carol Doak's Foundation Paper

HOW-TO

Use ¼" seam allowances.

> **TIP** If you are not familiar with paper piecing, try one of the following resources:
>
> · *Every Quilter's Foundation Piecing Reference Tool* by Jane Hall and Dixie Haywood
>
> · *Carol Doak Teaches You to Paper Piece* DVD

1. Make 4 copies of the triangle pattern using the foundation pattern (page 209). Paper piece the 4 triangles, adding the pieces in numerical order. Refer to the block photo (page 50) for color placement.

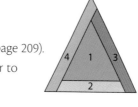

2. With right sides together, sew the A and B triangles to the foundation-pieced triangles to create the top half of the block. Repeat to assemble the bottom half of the block.

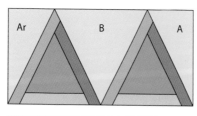

3. With right sides together, sew the upper half of the block to the lower half, carefully aligning the points. Press the seam open.

4. Trim the block to 12½" × 12½".

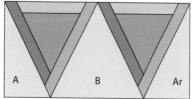

designed by Natasha Bruecher

DRUNKARD'S **BULL'S EYE**

This block is a combination of quarter-circles and half-square triangles.

Don't be afraid of circles—they are much easier than you think,

especially if you break the circle into quarter-circles.

SUPPLIES AND CUTTING

Template patterns are on page 214.

White fabric

Cut 2 squares 3⅞″ × 3⅞″.

Cut 8 pieces using Template C.

Light gray print fabric

Cut 4 pieces using Template C.

Cut 8 quarter-circles using Template A.

Pink fabric

Cut 8 arcs using Template B.

Cut 2 quarter-circles using Template A.

Yellow print fabric

Cut 4 arcs using Template B.

Dark gray print fabric

Cut 2 squares 3⅞″ × 3⅞″.

Cut 2 quarter-circles using Template A.

HOW-TO

Use ¼″ seam allowances.

1. Make 2 half-square triangles using a 3⅞″ × 3⅞″ white square and a 3⅞″ × 3⅞″ dark gray print square (see Half-Square Triangle Units, page 27). Repeat to make a total of 4 half-square triangles. Set aside.

2. Pin a pink arc B to a white C, matching the center first and then the ends. Stitch the curved seam. Press the seam allowance toward C.

3. Pin a light gray quarter-circle A to the unit from Step 2, matching the center and ends. Stitch the curved seam and press the seam allowance toward B. Trim the unit to 3½″ × 3½″.

4. Repeat Steps 2 and 3 to make 8 units.

5. Repeat Steps 2 and 3 to make 2 units with a light gray C, a yellow arc B, and a pink quarter-circle A.

6. Repeat Steps 2 and 3 to make 2 units with a light gray C, a yellow arc B, and a dark gray print quarter-circle A.

7. Arrange the units into 4 rows as shown, with the half-square triangles from Step 1 placed in the corners. Sew the units into rows. Sew the rows together to complete the block. Press. Trim the block, if necessary, to 12½″ × 12½″.

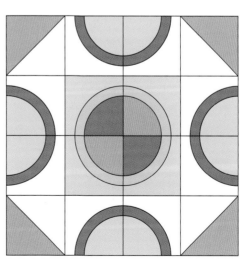

ECCENTRIC
designed by
Wayne Kollinger

WONKY STAR

Repeat, rotate, or reflect this block to create exciting designs.

SUPPLIES AND CUTTING

Enlarge the pattern (page 210) by 200%. Use an ultra-fine-point permanent marking pen to trace the pattern onto the shiny side of freezer paper. Carefully cut the freezer paper apart to create the templates. Iron the freezer paper onto the back of each fabric and cut out, adding an exact ¼" seam allowance to all sides of each piece.

6" × 13" green fabric

Cut B3 and B4.

3" × 22" dark green fabric

Cut B2, C1, and A6.

10" × 22" tan fabric

Cut A1, A4, A5, B1, B5, C2, C3, and C6.

8" × 9" brown fabric

Cut C4 and C5.

3" × 10" dark brown fabric

Cut A2 and A3.

Freezer paper

Ultra-fine-point permanent marking pen

HOW-TO

Use ¼" seam allowances.

1. Arrange all the pieces as shown. Check that they are all there and cut correctly.

2. Either leave the freezer paper on the back of the fabric and use the edge of the freezer paper as your sewing line, or draw the seamline on the wrong side of each piece.

3. With right sides together, pair up the pieces and poke pins through the points to ensure that they line up. Sew the triangles together to make square and rectangular units as shown. Press the seams open to reduce bulk.

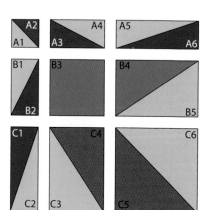

4. Sew the units into rows. Press.

5. Sew the rows together. Press. Remove freezer paper, if you have not done so already.

6. Trim the block to 12½" × 12½".

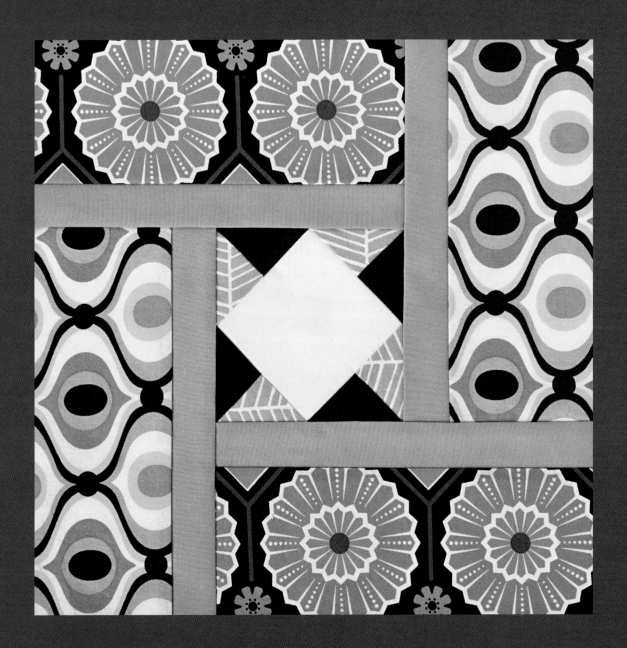

ENVY
designed by Angela Pingel

The center square is the special part of this block, and it's best to use three fabrics that contrast sharply with one another. The alternate colors in the triangles give motion to the block, so consider these options carefully.

SUPPLIES AND CUTTING

White fabric

Cut 1 square 3⅜" × 3⅜" (D).

Light blue print fabric

Cut 1 square 3¼" × 3¼"; then cut on the diagonal twice (C1).

Dark blue solid fabric

Cut 1 square 3¼" × 3¼"; then cut on the diagonal twice (C2).

Large floral fabric

Cut 2 strips 3½" × 8½" (you may want to cut these directionally) (A1).

Large print fabric

Cut 2 strips 3½" × 8½" (you may want to cut these directionally) (A2).

Green solid fabric

Cut 4 strips 1½" × 8½" (B).

HOW-TO

Use ¼" seam allowances.

1. With right sides together, place C2 on C1 with short sides aligned. Sew and press the seam toward C1. Make 4.

2. Mark the center of each side of the D square. With right sides together, center a C1/C2 triangle on 1 side of D and sew. Press away from the center. Repeat to complete the center square. Trim the overhanging tips from the C triangles. Square to 4½" × 4½".

3. Arrange the A1, A2, and B strips around the center of the block.

4. With right sides together, sew together the A's and B's. If using directional fabrics for A, be sure to pay attention to which pieces are sewn together.

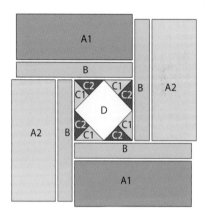

5. With right sides together, sew the center square to the upper right edge of the first segment, stopping midway with a backstitch to make a partial seam.

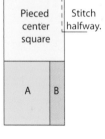

6. Sew the remaining segments around the center square in a clockwise direction. Press all the seams away from the center square.

7. Complete the partial seam between the first segment and the center square.

8. Trim the block to 12½" × 12½".

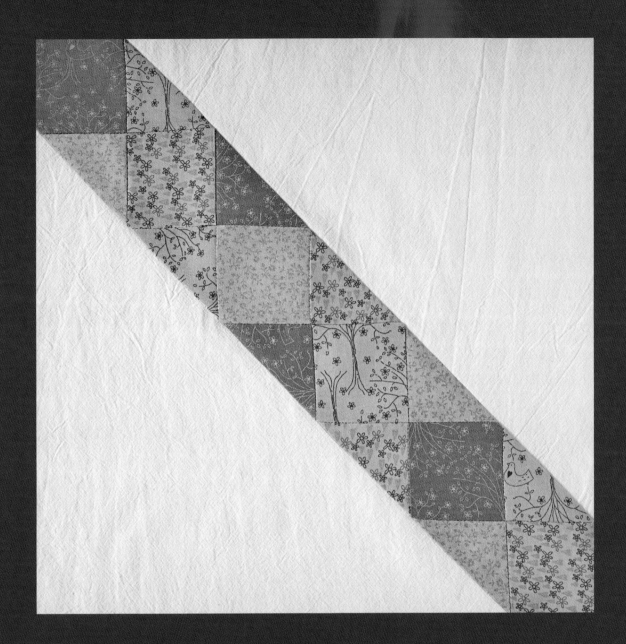

ESCALATOR
designed by
Ann Haley

This block pairs earthy updated pastels with a crinkly muslin.
Alternating the orientation of the diagonal strip with multiple blocks
in a quilt provides dynamic design options.

SUPPLIES AND CUTTING

Muslin fabric

Cut 1 square 11″ × 11″; and then cut in half on the diagonal.

Brown print fabric

Cut 2 squares 2½″ × 2½″.

Cut 1 square 2⅞″ × 2⅞″; and then cut in half on the diagonal.

Pink print fabric

Cut 2 squares 2½″ × 2½″.

Cut 1 square 2⅞″ × 2⅞″; and then cut in half on the diagonal.

Blue print fabric

Cut 1 square 2½″ × 2½″.

Cut 2 squares 2⅞″ × 2⅞″; and then cut in half on the diagonal.

Green print fabric

Cut 1 square 2½″ × 2½″.

Cut 2 squares 2⅞″ × 2⅞″; and then cut in half on the diagonal.

HOW-TO

Use ¼″ seam allowances.

1. Arrange the brown, pink, blue, and green squares and triangles in rows. Sew together as shown.

2. Sew the rows together, matching the seams to create the diagonal strip.

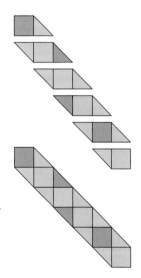

3. With right sides together, center and pin a muslin triangle to one side of the pieced diagonal strip. Sew with the diagonal strip facing up, removing the pins as you approach them. Press the seam toward the pieced strip.

4. With right sides together, center, pin, and sew a muslin triangle to the other side of the pieced diagonal strip. Press the seam toward the strip.

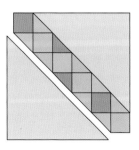

5. Press and trim the block to 12½″ × 12½″.

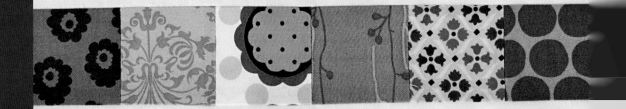

designed by **Louise Papas**

EVERYTHING **EQUAL**

This is a versatile, easy block and a fun project for using up those endless scraps.
For a great modern look, add some white, your favorite colored solid,
or a lovely linen background.

SUPPLIES AND CUTTING

White linen fabric

Cut 2 strips 12½" × 3½".

Cut 1 strip 12½" × 2½".

Pink fabric scraps

Cut 12 squares 2½" × 2½".

HOW-TO

1. With right sides together, sew 6 pink squares together in a row. Press the seams to one side. Repeat with the other 6 pink squares to make 2 rows of 6 squares each.

2. With right sides together, sew the pink pieced rows to the top and bottom of the 12½" × 2½" white strip. Press the seams toward the darker fabrics.

3. Sew 12½" × 3½" white strips to the top and bottom of the center unit. Press.

4. Trim the block to 12½" × 12½".

EXUBERANT
designed by
Susan Brubaker Knapp

This needle-turn appliqué block captures the exuberance of one of my favorite summer flowers—the zinnia. Batiks and hand-dyed fabrics make the flower look more naturalistic. I stitched this block using needle-turn appliqué, but you could do it with fused fabric and a satin stitch.

SUPPLIES AND CUTTING

Template patterns are on pages 210 and 211.

White fabric

Cut 1 square 14″ × 14″. Trim to 12½″ × 12½″ after appliqué.

Green fabric

Cut 4 bias strips 1″ × 8½″ for A.

Pink fabric 1

Cut 8 B petals.*

Pink fabric 2

Cut 8 C petals.*

Pink fabric 3

Cut 8 D petals.*

Pink fabric 4

Cut 8 E petals.*

Cut 1 G flower center.*

Pink fabric 5

Cut 8 F petals.*

Cut 4 I stars.*

Orange/yellow fabric

Cut 12 H circles.*

Medium-weight clear vinyl

Cut 1 square 14″ × 14″.

Water-erasable marker

¼″-wide bias bars

Variegated yellow perle cotton or embroidery floss

* Add a ¼″ seam allowance for needle-turn appliqué.

HOW-TO

1. Enlarge the placement diagram by 400%.

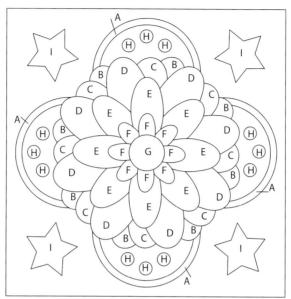

Placement diagram—enlarge 400%.

2. Make a positioning overlay by placing vinyl on top of the enlarged placement diagram and tracing all the lines, including the block outline, using a fine-point permanent marker.

3. With a water-erasable marker, draw a 12″ × 12″ square centered on the 14″ × 14″ white fabric.

4. Tape the 14″ × 14″ white background fabric to a flat surface. Place the vinyl positioning overlay on top of the white fabric, aligning the block outline. Tape the top edge of the positioning overlay to the top edge of the fabric square.

5. Use a bias bar to make 4 bias vines that are ¼″ × 8½″. Use the overlay to position the vines on the white background fabric. Pin the vines with appliqué pins; then appliqué along each edge.

6. Using the overlay, position the small circles and stars; then appliqué.

7. In a similar manner, appliqué the petals in place, working from the outer petals to the center circle, as shown in the block photo (page 62).

8. Embroider small star shapes around the perimeter of the center circle.

9. Press the block and trim to 12½″ × 12½″.

designed by Melissa Crow

FEATHERED **FRIENDS**

This whimsical block makes a perfect centerpiece for a smaller art quilt.
Or use these lovebirds as inspiration to create a series of scenes appliquéd on natural
linen for a showstopping full-size quilt. Experiment with your own color combinations
and with the positions of the birds and banners. Personalize the block
by making the birds say whatever you like.

SUPPLIES AND CUTTING

To create appliqué patterns, trace the designs from the block photo (page 64) and enlarge by 200%.

Notes: Appliqué and embroidery work may be easiest with the linen fabric securely attached to an embroidery hoop. If your finished quilt will be laundered, be sure to prewash the wool felt.

Natural linen fabric

Cut 1 square 14″ × 14″. Trim to 12½″ × 12½″ after appliqué.

Brown, olive green, light green, teal, blue, and white wool felt

Cut appliqué shapes as needed using the enlarged designs. (Do not add a turn-under allowance when cutting shapes from wool felt.)

Embroidery floss in white, brown, and burgundy

HOW-TO

1. Use the block photo (page 64) as a reference to position the appliqué shapes in the center of the linen square. Stitch the branch, banners, and birds in place using matching thread. Leave part of the wings, tails, and banner ends unstitched for added dimension.

2. With 2 strands of embroidery floss, stitch the words and banner strings using a backstitch. Add the leaves with a backstitch along the center veins only.

3. Use a French knot to add an eye to each bird.

4. Trim the block to 12½″ × 12½″.

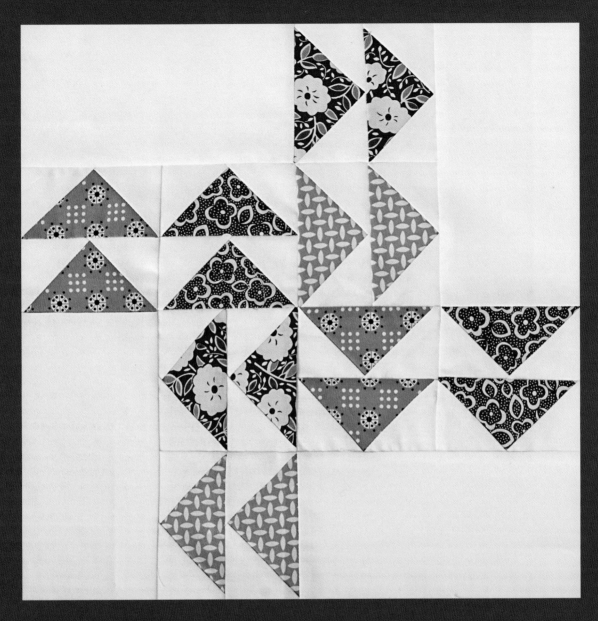

designed by Sherri McConnell

FOLLOW THE **LEADER**

This block uses traditional Flying Geese units in a whimsical setting.
All sixteen geese units can be made with unique fabrics, or different combinations
of fabrics can be used to achieve a more structured look.

SUPPLIES AND CUTTING

White fabric

Cut 4 rectangles 3½″ × 6½″.

Cut 32 squares 2″ × 2″.

Green fabric

Cut 4 rectangles 2″ × 3½″.

Red fabric

Cut 4 rectangles 2″ × 3½″.

Dark blue fabric

Cut 4 rectangles 2″ × 3½″.

Light blue fabric

Cut 4 rectangles 2″ × 3½″.

HOW-TO

Use ¼″ seam allowances.

1. Create a Flying Geese unit using 2 white
2″ × 2″ squares and 1 green 2″ × 3½″ rectangle (see
Flying Geese instructions, at right). Repeat to make
4 green, 4 red, 4 dark blue, and 4 light blue Flying
Geese units.

2. Join 2 Flying Geese units of the
same color as shown. Press. Make
8 pairs.

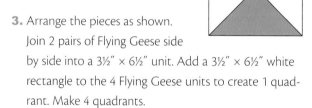

3. Arrange the pieces as shown.
Join 2 pairs of Flying Geese side
by side into a 3½″ × 6½″ unit. Add a 3½″ × 6½″ white
rectangle to the 4 Flying Geese units to create 1 quadrant. Make 4 quadrants.

4. Join the quadrants as shown to complete the block.
Press.

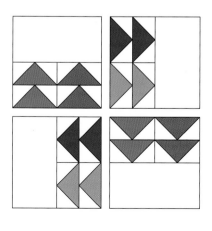

FLYING GEESE

*Refer to the project instructions
for the sizes of the squares and
rectangles.*

1. Lightly draw a diagonal
line from one corner
to the opposite
corner on the wrong
sides of 2 squares.

2. With right
sides
together,
place a
square on
one end of
the rect-
angle. Sew directly on the line,
trim the seam allowance to ¼″,
and press open.

3. With right
sides
together,
place the
other
square on
the other
end of the rectangle. Sew directly
on the line, trim the seam allowance to ¼″, and press open.

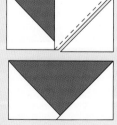

FOUR ACRES
designed by
Solidia Hubbard

This block is a twist on the traditional Log Cabin. Once the Log Cabin block is made, it is cut into four equal pieces and reassembled with sashing and a border. Using all solids or Christmas-themed fabrics would be beautiful.

SUPPLIES AND CUTTING

White fabric

Cut 1 square 4″ × 4″ for the Log Cabin center.

Cut 2 strips 10″ × 1¾″ for the border.

Cut 2 strips 13″ × 1¾″ for the border.

Jade fabric

Cut 1 strip 1½″ × 4″ for a log.

Cut 2 strips 1½″ × 5″ for logs.

Cut 1 strip 1½″ × 6″ for a log.

Periwinkle fabric

Cut 1 strip 1½″ × 6″ for a log.

Cut 2 strips 1½″ × 7″ for logs.

Cut 1 strip 1½″ × 8″ for a log.

Emerald fabric

Cut 1 strip 1″ × 8″ for a log.

Cut 2 strips 1″ × 8½″ for logs.

Cut 1 strip 1″ × 9″ for a log.

Blush fabric

Cut 2 strips 2″ × 4½″ for the sashing.

Cut 1 strip 2″ × 10″ for the sashing.

HOW-TO

Use ¼″ seam allowances.

1. With right sides together, add the jade fabric strips to the white 4″ × 4″ square center. Press as you go.

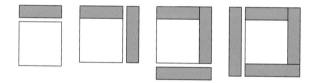

2. Add the periwinkle and emerald strips in the same manner to complete the Log Cabin.

3. Square up the Log Cabin unit from Step 2 to 9″ × 9″.

4. Cut the Log Cabin unit into 4 equal squares 4½″ × 4½″ each.

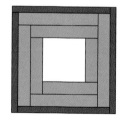

5. With right sides together, sew the squares from Step 4 to the sashing as shown. Press as you go.

6. Add a 10″ × 1¾″ white strip to either side of the unit from Step 5. Press. Add 13″ × 1¾″ white strips to the top and bottom and press. Trim the block to 12½″ × 12½″.

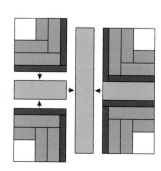

designed by Jessica Brown

FRACTURED **TRIANGLES**

This block is a study in scale. The complex piecing of one half
is tempered by the simplicity of the other. Chain piecing the components
for multiple blocks would certainly speed up the construction.
Tiny half-square triangles are a great way to use up scraps!

SUPPLIES AND CUTTING

Magenta fabric

Cut 6 squares 2⅜″ × 2⅜″.

Cut 1 square 3⅞″ × 3⅞″.

Cut 5 squares 2″ × 2″.

Cut 3 squares 3½″ × 3½″.

Yellow fabric

Cut 6 squares 2⅜″ × 2⅜″.

Cut 1 square 3⅞″ × 3⅞″

Cut 1 square 2″ × 2″.

Cut 1 square 13″ × 13″. Cut in half on the diagonal.

HOW-TO

Use ¼″ seam allowances. Press all the seams open, unless otherwise specified.

1. Place a 2⅜″ × 2⅜″ magenta square and a 2⅜″ × 2⅜″ yellow square right sides together to make 2 half-square triangles (page 27). Repeat to make 12 magenta and yellow half-square triangles.

2. Place the 3⅞″ × 3⅞″ magenta square and the 3⅞″ × 3⅞″ yellow square right sides together and make 2 half-square triangles.

3. With right sides together, sew the units together as shown. Press.

4. With right sides together, sew the 4 columns together. Press (some seams may be difficult to press open; press to one side as necessary).

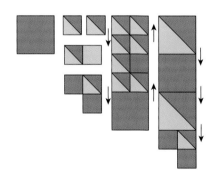

5. With right sides together, place a large yellow triangle on the pieced unit, matching the short sides. Pin carefully to prevent shifting.

6. Sew from corner to corner, taking care not to sew past the unit seam allowances to avoid cutting off triangle points.

7. Trim the magenta waste from the pieced unit. Press the block open and square to 12½″ × 12½″.

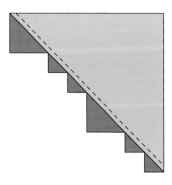

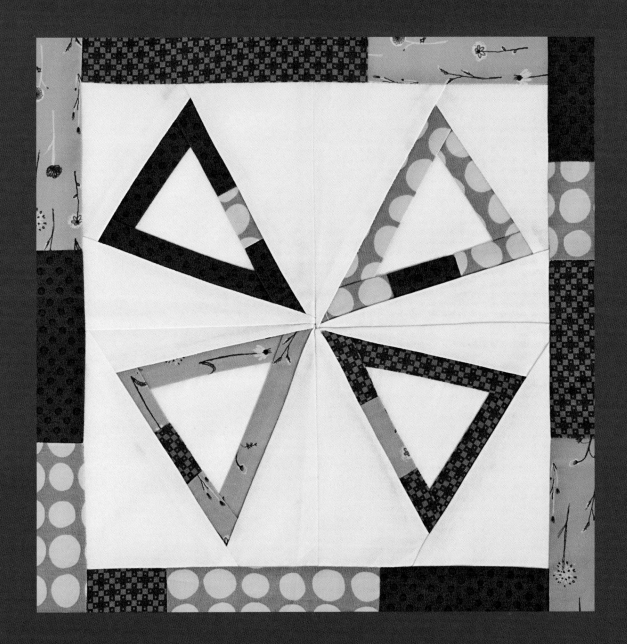

FREEWHEELING
designed by
Natasha Bruecher

This block is made using paper piecing. But don't be put off. This is a very simple block and is quick and easy to sew up. It is a great introduction to paper piecing for those of you who might be new to the technique.

SUPPLIES AND CUTTING

White fabric

Cut 8 squares 6″ × 6″. Cut each square in half on the diagonal.

Green fabric

Cut 6 strips 1½″ × 6″.

Cut 2 strips 1½″ × 2″

Cut 2 strips 1½″ × 15″.

Plum fabric

Cut 6 strips 1½″ × 6″.

Cut 2 strips 1½″ × 2″.

Cut 2 strips 1½″ × 15″.

Freezer paper, 10″ × 10″

HOW-TO

TIP If you are not familiar with paper piecing, try one of the following resources:

· *Every Quilter's Foundation Piecing Reference Tool* by Jane Hall and Dixie Haywood

· *Carol Doak Teaches You to Paper Piece* DVD

1. Cut the freezer paper into 4 squares, each 5″ × 5″. On the dull side of the paper, draw a triangle so that one

of the points touches one corner of the square. Use a ruler to draw another triangle ½″ inside the first triangle. Have fun with the shape of the triangles.

2. Extend the lines on the inner triangle to break the triangle outline into 3 different sections. Extend the lines on the outer triangle to break the background square into 3 sections. Number the sections in each square as shown.

3. Place a white fabric triangle right side up over the inner triangle (1) on the shiny side of the freezer paper, making sure it extends past the triangle by at least ¼″ on all sides. Hold the freezer paper up to a light source to see the triangle lines through the paper. Use your iron to temporarily tack the middle of the fabric in place. Trim to ¼″ larger than the drawn triangle on all sides.

4. Start by sewing section 2 in place. Line up a green

1½″ × 6″ strip along the edge of the white triangle on section 2, right sides facing. Make sure the ends of the strip overlap the ends of the white triangle. Sew on the line. Fold back the strip and press in place on the freezer paper.

5. Repeat to add another green strip to section 3.

6. Cut a green 1½″ × 6″ strip into 2 pieces. Insert a plum 1½″ × 2″ strip between the 2 green pieces and sew them back together into 1 strip.

7. Repeat Step 4 for section 4 using the pieced green and plum strip from Step 6.

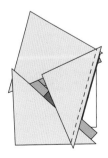

8. Trim the green strips ¼″ outside the outer triangle. Sew 3 of the white triangles in place over sections 5, 6, and 7. Allow the white fabric to extend past the edges of the paper square by more than ¼″.

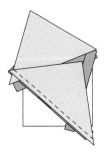

– – – – – Continued on page 206 – – – – –

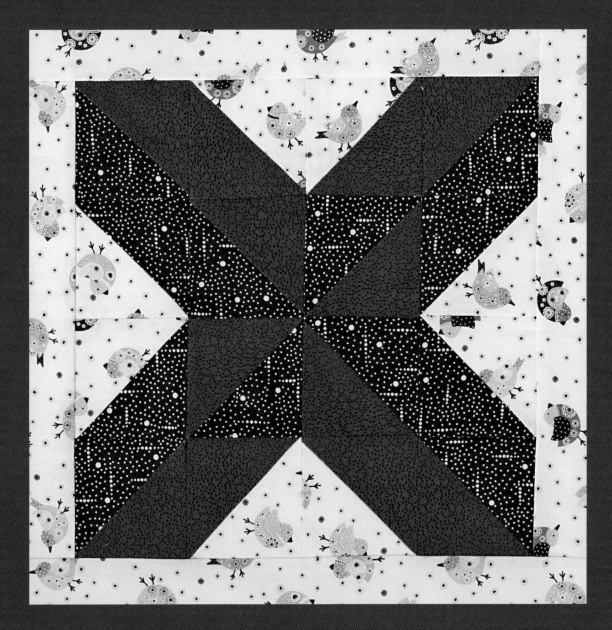

designed by Monika Wintermantel

FRONT AND **CENTER**

This is a powerful block. I love the different effect of the block
when you switch the colors. You can easily change the pattern
by changing the arrangement of the half-square triangles.

SUPPLIES AND CUTTING

Bird print fabric for background

Cut 4 squares 3½″ × 3½″; and then cut in half on the diagonal.

Cut 4 strips 1½″ × 13″.

Gray fabric

Cut 6 squares 3½″ × 3½″; and then cut in half on the diagonal.

Red fabric

Cut 6 squares 3½″ × 3½″; and then cut in half on the diagonal.

HOW-TO

Use ¼″ seam allowances.

1. Pair the triangles as follows:

8 pairs gray and red triangles

4 pairs bird and gray triangles

4 pairs bird and red triangles

2. With right sides together, sew the pairs on the diagonal using a ¼″ seam to make half-square triangles. Be careful not to stretch the fabrics. Press the seams toward the darker fabric. Trim each half-square triangle to 3″ × 3″.

3. Arrange the half-square triangles as shown.

4. With right sides together, sew the units into rows. Press the seams in Row 1 to the left, Row 2 to the right, Row 3 to the left, and Row 4 to the right.

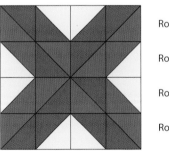

Row 1

Row 2

Row 3

Row 4

5. With right sides together, sew the rows together. Press the seams open (they will be flatter this way).

6. Trim the block center to 10½″ × 10½″ if needed.

7. With right sides together, sew a 1½″ × 13″ print strip to one side of the square. Trim the excess from the ends. Press the seam toward the strip. Repeat to add a print strip to each remaining side of the block center. Trim the block to 12½″ × 12½″.

FUNGUS FAMILY
PORTRAIT
designed by
Amy Sinibaldi

This simple block will allow you to showcase your favorite fabrics.
Experiment with different combinations of prints for the mushrooms and bright colors
that will really pop out from the linen background.

SUPPLIES AND CUTTING

Linen fabric

Cut 1 square 7" × 7".

Cut 2 strips 2¾" × 8".

Cut 2 strips 2¾" × 12½".

Green floral fabric

Cut 2 strips 1" × 7".

Cut 2 strips 1" × 8".

Assorted scraps
for mushroom appliqué

Paper-backed fusible web

HOW-TO

Use ¼" seam allowances.

1. With right sides together, sew the 1" × 7" green strips to the left and right sides of the 7" × 7" linen square. Press toward the green fabric. Sew the 1" × 8" green strips to the top and bottom of the linen square. Press toward the green fabric.

2. With right sides together, sew the 2¾" × 8" linen strips to the left and right sides of the block center and press toward the green fabric. Sew the 2¾" × 12½" linen strips to the top and bottom of the block. Press toward the green fabric. Square the block to 12½" × 12½".

3. Trace the designs from the block photo (page 76) and enlarge by 200%. Reverse the images and trace the mushroom shapes onto the paper side of the fusible web. Cut them out with a ½" margin all around.

4. Following the manufacturer's directions, iron the fusible web onto the back of the mushroom fabrics. Cut out the fabric shapes on the drawn lines.

5. Remove the paper backing from the fabric appliqué pieces. Arrange the mushrooms on the block and fuse them in place.

6. Stitch twice around each mushroom in black thread using a wobbly, uneven stitch, close to the edge.

FUSSY **CUT**

designed by
Susanne Woods

Have fun selecting a focus fabric for this block.
Easy piecing and a 2½″ precut roll would make this a quick quilt
to make in a weekend.

SUPPLIES AND CUTTING

Owl fabric

Fussy cut 7 squares 2½″ × 2½″.

Cream fabric

Cut 4 squares 2½″ × 2½″ (A).

Cut 4 rectangles 4½″ × 2½″ (B).

Cut 2 rectangles 6½″ × 2½″ (C).

Brown leaf fabric

Cut 1 square 2½″ × 2½″ (D).

Cut 2 rectangles 4½″ × 2½″ (E).

Cut 1 rectangle 2½″ × 6½″ (F).

Squiggles fabric

Cut 1 square 2½″ × 2½″ (G).

Cut 1 rectangle 4½″ × 2½″ (H).

HOW-TO

1. With right sides together, sew the pieces into units as shown, pressing after each seam.

Unit 1   Unit 2   Unit 3   Unit 4

2. With right sides together, sew units together as shown. Press.

Unit 1   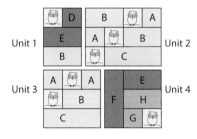   Unit 2

Unit 3   Unit 4

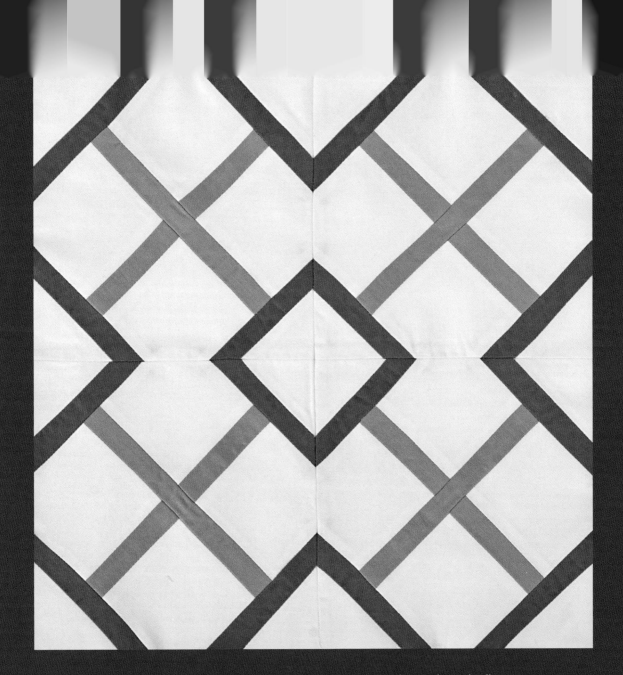

designed by Weeks Ringle and Bill Kerr

GARDEN **LATTICE**

Garden Lattice creates an on-point look with blocks that are not actually diagonal.
Using just two colors for the lattice brings a crisp modern aesthetic. You could create
an equally graphic quilt by using just one color. Or mix up hundreds of strips
divided into lights and darks for a scrappy feel.

SUPPLIES AND CUTTING

White fabric

Cut 4 squares 6½″ × 6½″.

Light green fabric

Cut 8 strips 1″ × 6½″.

Dark green fabric

Cut 16 strips 1″ × 4½″.

HOW-TO

Use ¼″ seam allowances.

1. Measure in 2½″ from each corner of a 6½″ × 6½″ white square and make a mark.

2. Cut diagonally from mark to mark. Do not discard the corners.

3. Cut the center piece on the diagonal through the center (find the center by folding it in half diagonally).

4. With right sides together, insert a 1″ × 6½″ light green strip between the 2 halves. Trim the ends flush with the square. Press the seams open.

5. Cut the center piece on the diagonal through the center in the other direction.

6. With right sides together, insert a 1″ × 6½″ light green strip between the 2 halves. Trim the ends flush. Press the seams open.

7. With right sides together, add a 1″ × 4½″ dark green strip and corner to each corner of the square. Trim the ends flush and press the seams open.

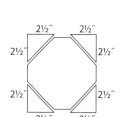

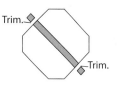

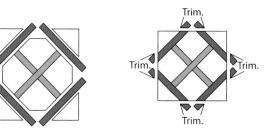

8. Repeat Steps 1–7 for the 3 remaining squares.

9. With right sides together, sew together the 4 squares to form the finished block, as shown in the block photo (page 80).

GNOME **HOME** designed by Solidia Hubbard

I chose to make my gnome a two-story home with a nice yard. Use your imagination and make an entire neighborhood filled with houses of all shapes and sizes. Perhaps Little Red Riding Hood will live next door to Snoopy! This would make a great "I Spy" quilt for your little one. Just fill the doorway with any patterned fabric you like.

SUPPLIES AND CUTTING

14" × 14" white fabric for background and windows

7" × 10" wood-grain print fabric for roof and tree trunks

5" × 5" green-and-red floral fabric for treetops

8" × 8" pink print fabric for house

2" × 3" gnome print fabric for gnome standing in doorway

4" × 13" green floral for grass

Freezer paper

HOW-TO

Enlarge the template pattern (page 211) by 200% before tracing onto freezer paper.

1. Trace the enlarged pattern onto the paper side of the freezer paper and cut apart the pieces. Iron the freezer paper pieces shiny side down on the right side of the fabrics, leaving enough space between them to add a ¼" seam allowance on all sides. Cut each piece from the fabric, adding a ¼" seam allowance.

2. With right sides together, sew together the pieces as shown, pressing as you go. Trim the block to 12½" × 12½".

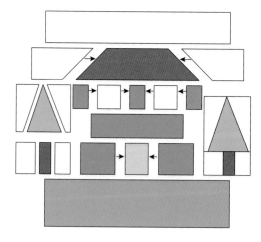

designed by Kate Henderson

HIGGLEDY-**PIGGLEDY**

This block is made of rectangles of different sizes and colors. When laying out an entire quilt, turn alternate blocks 90 degrees to create a steplike effect, or turn four blocks so they rotate around the same corner for a pinwheel effect.

SUPPLIES AND CUTTING

Green, gray, red, and blue fabrics

Cut 3 rectangles 2″ × 3½″ from each fabric.

Cut 1 rectangle 2½″ × 3½″ from each fabric.

Cut 1 rectangle 3″ × 3½″ from each fabric.

Cut 1 square 3½″ × 3½″ from each fabric.

HOW-TO

Use ¼″ seam allowances.

1. Arrange all the pieces as shown.

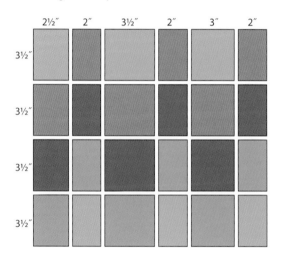

2. With right sides together, sew the pieces to form each row. Press the seam allowances in Rows 1 and 3 to the right. Press the seam allowances in Rows 2 and 4 to the left.

3. With right sides together, sew the rows together. Press.

designed by Monika Wintermantel

HOUSE ON THE **HILL**

Similar to Checkers (page 40), this is a great block for a bee group. Each member can add her own fabrics and show her creativity by adding an appliqué.

SUPPLIES AND CUTTING

Assorted print fabrics

Cut 20 squares 2″ × 2″ for the inner border.

Cut 16 squares 1¼″ × 1¼″ for the corner squares.

Tan fabric

Cut 1 square 6½″ × 6½″ for the appliqué background.

White fabric

Cut 4 strips 2″ × 9½″ for the outer border.

Fabric scraps for appliqué

Fusible web

HOW-TO

RAW-EDGE APPLIQUÉ

1. Trace the appliqué pieces from the block photo (page 86) and enlarge the drawing by 200%.

2. Reverse the shapes and trace them onto the paper side of the fusible web. Cut them out ¼″ outside the drawn lines.

3. Iron the cut-out shapes of fusible web onto the wrong side of the appliqué fabric, following the manufacturer's instructions. Cut out the fabric pieces on the drawn lines and peel off the backing paper.

4. Arrange and fuse the fabric pieces onto the tan square. Stitch around the shapes with black thread.

5. Machine stitch or embroider the grass on the hill and the smoke coming out of the chimney (see photo, previous page).

BORDERS

Use ¼″ seam allowances.

1. With right sides together, sew 4 squares 2″ × 2″ into a row. Press the seams in one direction. Repeat to make 2 sets of 4 squares.

2. With right sides together, sew 6 squares 2″ × 2″ into a row. Press the seams in one direction. Repeat to make 2 sets of 6 squares.

3. With right sides together, sew the 4-square rows from Step 1 to the top and bottom of the center square. Sew the 6-square rows from Step 2 to the sides of the center square. Press toward the pieced rows.

4. With right sides together, sew four 1¼″ × 1¼″ squares together to make a four-patch unit for a corner square. Repeat to make 4 four-patch units.

5. Sew 2″ × 9½″ white strips to the left and right sides of the block. Press.

6. Sew a four-patch unit from Step 4 to each end of the remaining 2″ × 9½″ white strips. Sew these strips to the top and bottom of the block. Press.

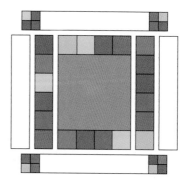

IN THE **HOOP** designed by Susanne Woods

Mimic an embroidery hoop hanging on the wall with this fun block.
Use a 7½″ embroidery design of your choice to showcase a special design or use
my leaf. I used C&T Transfer Artist Paper (TAP) to transfer the design onto the linen.

SUPPLIES AND CUTTING

Background fabric

Cut 1 square 12½" × 12½".

Linen fabric

Cut 1 square 11" × 11".

Wood-grain fabric

Cut 1 strip 1¼" × 35" on the bias.

Lightweight fusible stabilizer, such as Shape-Flex woven interfacing

Cut 1 square 11" × 11".

Embroidery floss in dark green

Perle cotton in bright green, pale green, and brown

Transfer Artist Paper (TAP)

HOW-TO

1. Iron fusible stabilizer to the back of the linen square.

2. Scan the leaf design from the block photo (page 88) and enlarge it 200%. Print the design on Transfer Artist Paper and iron it onto the linen square, or transfer the design onto the linen using your favorite method. Use a backstitch to embroider the design with perle cotton for the outer edge of the leaf, stem, and main veins. Embroider the thinner veins with 2 strands of floss using a backstitch.

3. Draw an 11"-diameter circle (I traced around a dinner plate) onto the linen and cut it out. Pin the circle on the center of the background fabric.

4. Fold the long edges of the 1¼"-wide wood-grain bias strip so they meet in the middle on the wrong side to form a ⅝" × 35" bias strip.

5. Pin the bias strip in a circle around the edge of the linen circle. Where the ends of the bias strip meet, fold under approximately ¼" and press. Topstitch the bias strip into place along the inner and outer edges.

IN THE **WINDOW** designed by Viv Wride

This block is a combination of pieced curves and regular straight piecing.
Fussy cutting the quarter-circles for the window can make this block look spectacular.

SUPPLIES AND CUTTING

Template patterns are on page 212.

Cream print fabric

Cut 4 quarter-circles using Template A.

Red solid fabric

Cut 4 arches using Template B.

Light green print fabric

Cut 4 rectangles 2½" × 7".

Cut 4 squares 2½" × 2½".

Dark green solid fabric

Cut 2 strips 3⅜" × 1¼".

Cut 3 strips 1¼" × 7".

Cut 2 strips 12½" × 1¼".

Cut 4 strips 1¼" × 2½".

HOW-TO

Use ¼" seam allowances and press after each step.

1. With right sides together, sew the curved edge of a cream quarter-circle A to the curved edge of a red arch B. Press the seam toward the arch. Repeat with the other 3 quarter-circles and arches.

2. With right sides together, sew a quarter-circle unit from Step 1 to the top and bottom of each 3⅜" × 1¼" dark green strip. Press toward the strip. Add a 1¼" × 7" dark green strip between the quarter-circle/strip units as shown. Press toward the center strip.

3. Add 1¼" × 7" dark green strips to either side of the center unit. Add 2½" × 7" light green strips to either side of the center unit. Press toward the dark green strip.

4. Add 12½" × 1¼" dark green strips to the top and bottom of the center unit. Press toward the dark green strips.

5. Sew a 1¼ × 2½" dark green strip to a 2½" × 2½" light green square to make a corner unit. Repeat to make 4 corner units. Press toward the dark green strips.

6. Add a corner unit to each end of a 2½" × 7" light green strip. Make 2. Sew one of the assembled strips to the top of the center unit and the other to the bottom to complete the block. Press toward the dark green strips. Trim the block to 12½" × 12½".

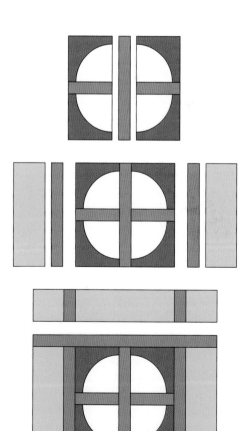

IT'S A **STRETCH** designed by Angela Pingel

This deceptively simple block is a spin-off of a traditional Courthouse Steps block. It is paper pieced in one large piece for accuracy, given the number of seams in one block. It looks just as lovely in other color combinations, and rotating the block in a quilt achieves a variety of patchwork patterns.

SUPPLIES AND CUTTING

⅛ yard or 1 fat quarter (18″ × 22″) black fabric

Cut as many 2″-wide strips as needed.

⅛ yard or 1 fat quarter (18″ × 22″), each of 4 purple fabrics in 4 different shades

Cut as many 2″-wide strips as needed.

Yellow fabric

Cut 1 strip 2½″ × 7½″.

Foundation paper, such as Simple Foundations Translucent Vellum Paper or Carol Doak's Foundation Paper

HOW-TO

> **TIP** If you are not familiar with paper piecing, try one of the following resources:
>
> · *Every Quilter's Foundation Piecing Reference Tool* by Jane Hall and Dixie Haywood
>
> · *Carol Doak Teaches You to Paper Piece* DVD

1. Enlarge the paper-piecing pattern (page 213) by 200% and check to make sure that the finished pattern measures 12″ × 12″.

2. Use your favorite paper-piecing technique to make this block. Use the block photo (page 92) as a guide and add the fabric strips in numerical order as indicated on the pattern. Press after adding each new piece for a crisp finish.

3. Trim the bock to 12½″ × 12½″ so that it extends ¼″ beyond the foundation pattern on all sides.

JUICY designed by Mo Beldell

Pick some juicy prints for the fruit and some contrasting prints
for the background. Yummy!

SUPPLIES AND CUTTING

Template patterns are on pages 212 and 213.

4 white-and-green print fabric scraps for background

Cut 4 using Template A.

4 pink print fabric scraps for fruit

Cut 4 using Template B.

Green fabric for outer strips and leaf

Cut 2 strips 8½″ × 2½″.

Cut 2 strips 12½″ × 2½″.

Cut 2 leaves using Template C.

Light green embroidery thread for leaf vein

HOW-TO

Use ¼″ seam allowances.

1. With right sides together, align the center marks of A and B. With B on top, pin well and sew. Notch the curve as needed. Sew all 4 quadrants. Press.

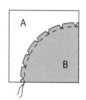

2. Using the project photo (page 94) as a reference and, with right sides together, sew the quadrants together. Press.

3. With right sides together, sew a 2½″ × 8½″ green strip to either side of the block. Press.

4. With right sides together, sew 2½″ × 12½″ green strips to the top and bottom of the block. Press.

5. With right sides together, pin the leaves (C) together and sew all around the edge, leaving a ¾″ opening for turning. Turn the leaf right side out and sew the opening shut. Press.

6. Using all 6 strands of the embroidery floss, sew a split stitch down the center of the leaf to create the veining.

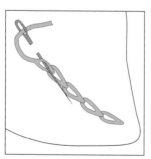

For split stitch, bring needle up through strands of previous stitch.

7. Hand stitch the leaf to the top center of the fruit, catching only the bottom layer of fabric so the stitches don't show on the front. Hand stitching along the vein on the back side of the leaf will also allow the edges of the leaf to remain free, adding a three-dimensional effect to the block.

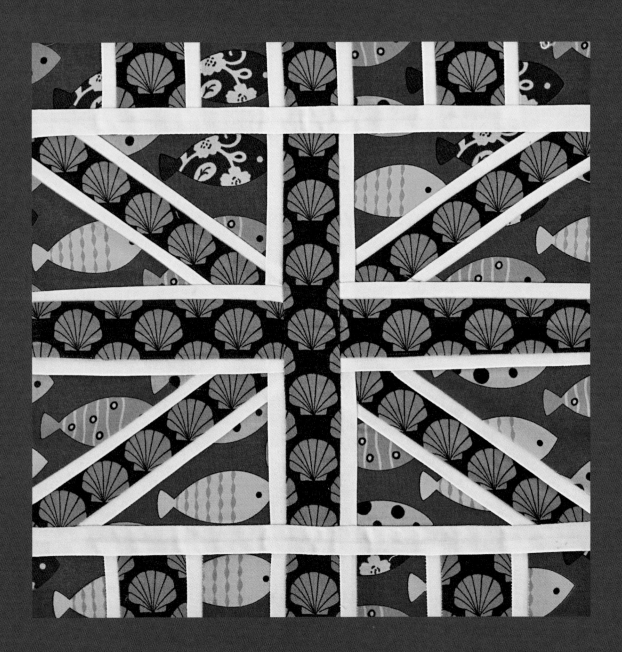

JUST **JACK** designed by Lynne Goldsworthy

This block uses a simplified version of the British Union Jack flag. It looks fabulous made up in all sorts of different plain or patterned fabrics. For maximum impact, make sure you have a good contrast between the fabrics that are shown as red and blue in my block and the skinny diagonal strips.

SUPPLIES AND CUTTING

Note: Experienced paper piecers may wish to fussy cut the fabrics for some or all of this block.

Red print fabric

Cut 2 strips 2″ × fabric width. Cut off lengths as you piece the block.

Blue print fabric

Cut 4 rectangles 6″ × 4¼″.
Cut 2 rectangles on the diagonal from top left to bottom right and 2 rectangles on the diagonal from top right to bottom left.
Cut 1 strip 2″ × 16″.

White fabric

Cut 3 strips 1″ × fabric width. Cut off lengths as you piece the block.

Foundation paper, such as Simple Foundations Translucent Vellum Paper or Carol Doak's Foundation Paper

HOW-TO

Use ¼″ seam allowances.

Enlarge the paper-piecing pattern (page 214) by 200% before using it.

> **TIP** If you are not familiar with paper piecing, try one of the following resources:
>
> · *Every Quilter's Foundation Piecing Reference Tool* by Jane Hall and Dixie Haywood
>
> · *Carol Doak Teaches You to Paper Piece* DVD

1. Copy or trace the enlarged pattern and cut apart sections A to G.

2. Paper piece each section, using small stitches (set your machine stitch length to around 1.5) and leaving a seam allowance of at least ¼″ around each template section.

3. Trim the seam allowances around each section to ¼″, change your stitch length back to whatever you normally use for piecing, and assemble the block as follows:

With right sides together, sew D to F and E to G, pressing the seams toward the middle wide stripe.

With right sides together, sew D/F to C and then E/G to C, taking care to align the horizontal stripe. Press the seams toward C.

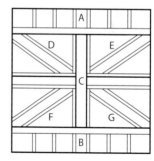

With right sides together, sew A to the top of the block and B to the bottom, taking care to align the vertical stripe. Press these seams toward A and B, respectively.

4. Trim the block to 12½″ × 12½″, leaving a ¼″ seam allowance beyond the foundation pattern on all sides. Carefully tear off all the paper from the back of the finished block. It should tear quite easily along the perforations made by the small stitches.

designed by Weeks Ringle and Bill Kerr

JUST PASSING **THROUGH**

There's an unexpected slyness to this design. You can make a quilt with this block by using just four fabrics. Or for a different look, you could have multiple palettes in play, mixing and matching. When the thin bands line up, the design will unify the blocks. Avoid fabrics with large-scale patterns that have too much contrast within the prints.

SUPPLIES AND CUTTING

Light orange fabric

Cut 6 rectangles 1½" × 3" (A).

Dark orange fabric

Cut 4 rectangles 2" × 3" (B).

Cut 4 rectangles 3½" × 3" (C).

Cut 2 rectangles 2" × 7½" (D).

Light purple fabric

Cut 3 rectangles 1½" × 7½" (E).

Dark purple fabric

Cut 4 rectangles 2" × 7½" (F).

HOW-TO

Use ¼" seam allowances.

1. With right sides together, sew the 3"-long dark (B and C) and light orange (A) pieces together into a row. Press the seams open. Repeat to make 2 rows.

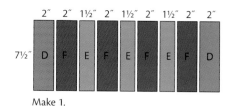

Make 2.

2. With right sides together, sew the 7½"-long strips of dark orange (D), dark purple (F), and light purple (E) together to make the center section of the block. Press the seams open.

Make 1.

3. Sew the orange rows to the top and bottom of the center section, pinning carefully to ensure that the seams match. Press the seams open.

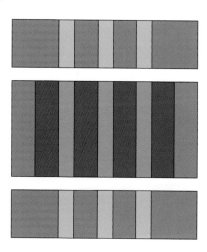

LAST **CALL**

designed by
Angela Pingel

The pieces that make up this block will probably look familiar. But this is a new ta
on a traditional pattern that uses a mixture of solids and prints, along with partial
completed circles, to fool the eye and keep it moving. Brush up on your curved
piecing and give this block a whirl.

SUPPLIES AND CUTTING

Template patterns are on page 209.

Variety of print and solid fabrics

Cut 16 using Template A.

Cut 16 using Template B.

HOW-TO

Use ¼" seam allowances.

1. Arrange the cut pieces to your liking, using the block photo (page 100) for reference.

2. Mark the center of each piece. With right sides together, align the center marks of A and B. With B on top, pin well and sew. Press toward A. Notch the curved seam as needed. Repeat to create 16 units.

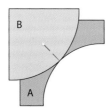 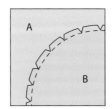

3. Arrange the units as shown in the block photo (page 100).

4. With right sides together, sew the units together into rows of 4 units. Press the seams of adjacent rows in opposite directions so the seams nest when the rows are sewn together.

5. With right sides together, sew the rows together.

6. Press and trim the block to 12½" × 12½".

designed by Latifah Saafir

LEMONS AND **LIMES**

Lemons come to life in a fresh way when you use this straightforward combination of squares and quarter-circles. This classic Sixteen-Patch block is made modern by the effective use of negative space, fabric selection, and four fun quarter-circles.

SUPPLIES AND CUTTING

Template patterns are on page 219.

White fabric

Cut 4 using Template A.

Cut 8 squares 3½″ × 3½″.

Pink fabrics

Cut 2 using Template B.

Green fabrics

Cut 2 using Template B.

Black fabrics

Cut 2 squares 3½″ × 3½″.

Gray fabrics

Cut 2 squares 3½″ × 3½″.

HOW-TO

Use ¼″ seam allowances.

1. Mark the centers of A and B. With right sides together, align the center marks of A and B. With B on top, pin well and sew. Notch the seams as needed. Press toward A. Square the unit to 3½″ × 3½″. Repeat to make 4 units.

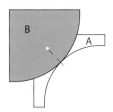
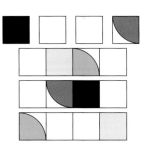

2. Arrange the 12 squares and 4 pieced units as shown. With right sides together, sew the squares into 4 rows.

3. Sew the 4 rows together to complete the block. Press and trim to 12½″ × 12½″.

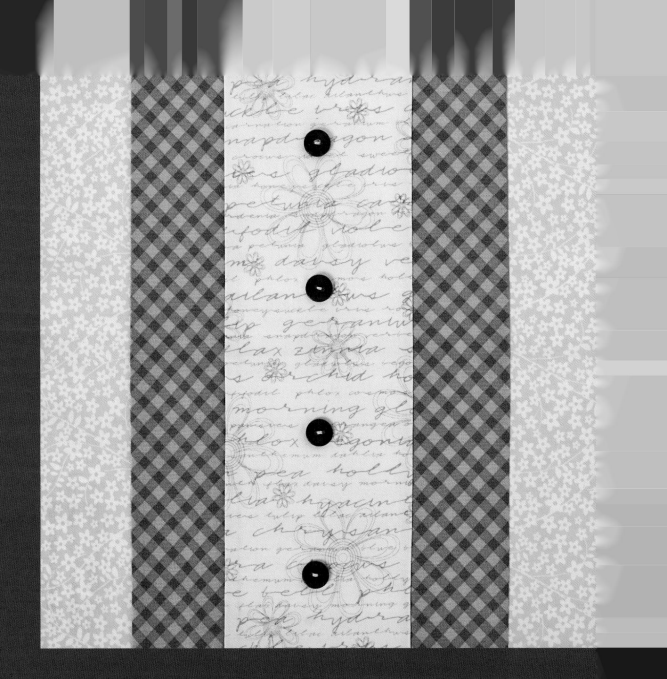

LINE **UP** designed by
Angela Yosten

This block was inspired by a tuxedo shirt with vertical tucks. This simple block can
made appropriate for any gender and generation with just a quick change of fabri
choice. Keep it simple with buttons, or add stitching embellishments.

SUPPLIES AND CUTTING

Cream print fabric

Cut 1 strip 4½″ × 12½″.

Pink fabric

Cut 2 strips 2½″ × 12½″.

Yellow fabric

Cut 2 strips 2½″ × 12½″.

HOW-TO

Use ¼″ seam allowances.

1. With right sides together, sew a pink strip on either side of the cream strip. Press toward the cream strip.

2. With right sides together, sew a yellow strip on either side of the unit created in Step 1. Press toward the pink strips.

3. Add buttons or stitching embellishments.

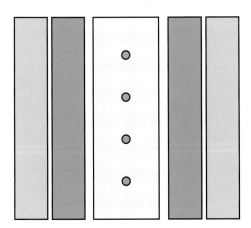

LINKS
designed by
John Q. Adams

This block is a breeze to make. When several are joined together,
they create a very modern and appealing chain-link effect. One set of instructions
yields two variations of the same block. Join several of these blocks together in
columns or rows for a very modern, very cohesive design.

SUPPLIES AND CUTTING

Focus fabric for center

Cut 1 square 6½" × 6½".

Print fabric for background

Cut 2 strips 2½" × 6½".

Cut 2 strips 2½" × 10½".

Cut 2 strips 1½" × 4½".

White fabric for border

Cut 2 strips 1½" × 10½".

Cut 2 strips 1½" × 3½".

Cut 2 strips 1½" × 5½".

HOW-TO

Use ¼" seam allowances.

1. With right sides together, sew 2½" × 6½" strips of the print background fabric to the left and right sides of the 6½" × 6½" center square. Press toward the background strips.

2. With right sides together, sew 2½" × 10½" strips of the print background fabric to the top and bottom of the assembled piece from Step 1. Press toward the background.

3. With right sides together, sew 1½" × 10½" strips of the white border fabric to the left and right sides of the assembled piece. Press toward the white border strips.

4. Join a 1½" × 3½" white border strip, a 1½" × 4½" print strip, and a 1½" × 5½" white strip, with right sides together. Make 2.

5. With right sides together, sew a border from Step 4 to the top of the block. Rotate the remaining border 180° and sew it to the bottom edge of the block. Refer to the block photo (page 106) for placement.

TIP For alternating blocks, simply flip the placement of the top and bottom borders. This allows you to link the alternating blocks to create a chain-link effect in each column of your quilt.

LITTLE SQUARE,
BIG SQUARE

designed by
Kim Schaefer

In any color combination, this block is a winner.

SUPPLIES AND CUTTING

Fabric 1

Cut 1 square 2½″ × 2½″ (A).

Fabric 2

Cut 2 rectangles 2½″ × 3½″ (B).

Cut 2 rectangles 3½″ × 8½″ (C).

Fabric 3

Cut 2 rectangles 1½″ × 8½″ (D).

Cut 2 rectangles 1½″ × 10½″ (E).

Fabric 4

Cut 2 rectangles 1½″ × 10½″ (F).

Cut 2 rectangles 1½″ × 12½″ (G).

HOW-TO

Use ¼″ seam allowances.

1. With right sides together, sew B rectangles to the left and right sides of A. Press.

2. With right sides together, sew C rectangles to the top and bottom of the unit from Step 1. Press.

3. With right sides together, sew D strips to the left and right sides of the unit from Step 2. Press.

4. With right sides together, sew E strips to the top and bottom of the block. Press.

5. With right sides together, sew F strips to the left and right sides of the block. Press.

6. With right sides together, sew G strips to the top and bottom of the block. Press. Trim the block to 12½″ × 12½″.

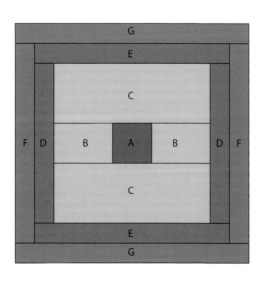

maybe...

MAYBE . . .

designed by
Susanne Woods

This block chronicles my decision-making process … in block form. Have fun addi

meaningful words of your own and using a color that is relevant to the mood of your c

If you are constructing an entire quilt from this one block, consider alternating the po

of the striped fabric within individual blocks to give the quilt movement.

SUPPLIES AND CUTTING

6 fabrics in different colors or values

Cut 1 strip 2¼″ × 12½″ from each
color or value.

Fabric with lines

Cut 1 strip 2¼″ × 12½″.

Lightweight fusible interfacing, such
as Shape-Flex woven interfacing

Cut 1 strip 2¼″ × 12½″.

Perle cotton in dark gray

HOW-TO

Use ¼″ seam allowances.

1. Iron the fusible interfacing to the back of the fabric with lines, following
the manufacturer's directions.

2. Embroider a word or words onto the lined fabric, leaving at least 1″
between the right edge of the strip and the end of your embroidery.

3. With right sides together, sew the strips together as shown in the block
photo (page 110). Press. Trim the block to 12½″ × 12½″.

MEGAN'S **STAR**
designed by
Alethea Ballard

This wonderful star floats in the middle of the block to make a stunning statement
in a quilt. It has a nice big center, which is perfect for a beautiful flower
or a cool conversation print. The corner triangles create a secondary pattern
that skips across the quilt and adds interest.

SUPPLIES AND CUTTING

Large-print fabric for center

Cut 1 square 4¾″ × 4¾″. (The flower in the center square of this block was fussy cut on the diagonal.)

Green fabric for center triangles

Cut 2 squares 4″ × 4″. Cut each square on the diagonal to create 4 triangles.

Dark pink fabric for star points

Cut 8 squares 2½″ × 2½″.

Light pink fabric for background

Cut 4 rectangles 1½″ × 3½″ (C).

Cut 8 rectangles 3½″ × 4½″ (A and B).

Green fabric for corner triangles

Cut 2 squares 2½″ × 2½″.

Aqua fabric for corner triangles

Cut 2 squares 2½″ × 2½″.

HOW-TO

Use ¼″ seam allowances.

1. With right sides together, sew 2 center triangles to opposite sides of the center square. Press and trim the seam allowances.

2. With right sides together, sew the remaining 2 center triangles to the other sides of the center square. Trim the seam allowances. Press and trim the square to 6½″ × 6½″.

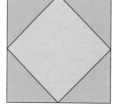

3. Draw a diagonal line from corner to corner on the wrong side of the 2½″ × 2½″ star points. With right sides together, place a square on a corner of the 3½″ × 4½″ background rectangle. Stitch on the line. Trim the excess and press open. Repeat on the other end of the B unit. Make 4 B units.

4. In a similar manner, draw a diagonal line from corner to corner on the wrong side of the 2½″ × 2½″ corner triangles. With right sides together, place a square on a corner of the 3½″ × 4½″ background rectangle. Stitch on the line. Trim the seam allowance and press open. Make 2 left A units with green fabric and 2 right A units with aqua fabric.

Make 2.   Make 2.

5. Assemble the block as shown and press well.

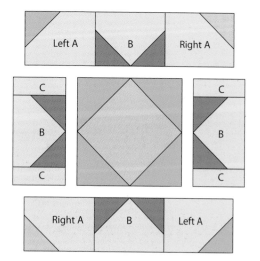

MEGAN'S STAR

designed by **Penny Michelle Layman**

MISSING YOUR **KISS**

This is actually a Nine-Patch block with a border. Try a solid, muted fabric for the background and brighter fabrics for the X's and the border.

SUPPLIES AND CUTTING

Linen fabric for background

Cut 1 square 4″ × 4″ for the center.

Cut 8 squares 4½″ × 4½″.

Fabric for X's

Cut 8 strips 14″ long, with the width of each strip tapering from ¾″ at one end to 1½″ at the other end.

Green fabric for border

Cut 2 strips 1¼″ × 10½″.

Cut 2 strips 1¼″ × 12½″.

HOW-TO

Use ¼″ seam allowances.

1. Cut each of the 4½″ × 4½″ background squares on the diagonal twice as shown.

2. With right sides together, sew a strip between 2 adjacent triangles from Step 1. Trim the ends of the strip near the block center. Repeat with the opposite adjacent triangles.

3. With right sides together, sew the 2 halves from Step 2 together, inserting a strip as you did in Step 2. Trim the unit to 4″ × 4″.

4. Repeat Steps 2 and 3 to create 8 pieced units.

5. Arrange the 4″ × 4″ plain square and the 8 pieced units to your liking. With right sides together, sew the blocks into 3 rows of 3 blocks each. Press. With right sides together, sew the rows together. Press.

6. With right sides together, sew 1¼″ × 10½″ border strips to the left and right sides of the block. Press. Sew 1¼″ × 12½″ strips to the top and bottom of the block. Press. Trim the block to 12½″ × 12½″.

MONDRIAN

designed by
Jamie Moilanen

This modern block is in the style of Piet Mondrian paintings. It uses a large focal square and narrow dark strips to mimic the famous artwork. The large solid focal square can be replaced by your favorite fussy-cut print fabric for a fun alternative, or try adding more solids to the block for a contemporary option.

SUPPLIES AND CUTTING

Light gray fabric

Cut 1 square 5″ × 5″ for the center (A).

Dark charcoal fabric
(1″ × 28½″ total)

Cut 2 strips 1″ × 5″ (B).

Cut 2 strips 1″ × 6″ (C).

Cut 2 strips 1″ × 2″ (D).

Cut 1 strip 1″ × 2½″ (E).

Cut 1 strip 1″ × 12½″ (F).

Light green print

Cut 2 rectangles 2″ × 3″ (G).

Cut 1 rectangle 3¼″ × 9″ (H).

Olive green fabric

Cut 2 rectangles 2″ × 3″ (I).

Cut 1 rectangle 2½″ × 9″ (J).

Bright green fabric

Cut 1 rectangle 9″ × 2¼″ (K).

Cut 1 strip 1″ × 8″ (L).

Striped fabric

Cut 1 rectangle 2½″ × 4½″ (M).

Dark orange fabric

Cut 1 rectangle 2″ × 8″ (N).

Light orange fabric

Cut 1 strip 1½″ × 12½″ (O).

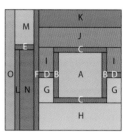

HOW-TO

Use ¼″ seam allowances.

1. With right sides together, sew a 1″ × 5″ dark charcoal strip B to either side of the 5″ × 5″ light gray center A. Press. Sew a 1″ × 6″ dark charcoal strip C to the top and bottom. Press.

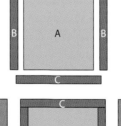

2. With right sides together, sew a 1″ × 2″ dark charcoal strip D between a 2″ × 3″ light green rectangle G and a 2″ × 3″ olive green rectangle I. Repeat to make 2 units. Sew a unit to either side of the center unit as shown.

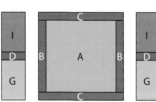

– – – – – Continued on page 206 – – – – –

designed by Rachel Roxburgh

MOUSE IN THE **HOUSE**

This block is a simple combination of squares, rectangles, appliqué, and a little embroidery. Linen placed against cotton fabrics and embellished with different appliqué techniques and embroidery combine to create a wonderful play with textures.

SUPPLIES AND CUTTING

Trace the appliqué and embroidery designs from the block photo (page 118) and enlarge by 200%.

Linen fabric A

Cut 1 rectangle 7″ × 8″ for the center.

Fabrics B, C, D, and E

Cut 1 square 3″ × 3″ of each fabric.

Fabric F

Cut 1 rectangle 1½″ × 8″.

Fabric G

Cut 1 rectangle 2½″ × 10½″.

Fabric H

Cut 1 rectangle 8″ × 1½″.

Fabric I

Cut 1 rectangle 2″ × 8″.

Fabric J

Cut 1 rectangle 12½″ × 2½″.

Scrap fabrics

Cut 1 elephant body (no seam allowance necessary).

Cut 1 elephant ear (add a seam allowance for needle-turn appliqué).

Paper-backed fusible web

Perle cotton thread in brown, blue, and sage green

TIP Reverse the appliqué designs if you wish the elements to face in the opposite direction.

HOW-TO

Use ¼″ seam allowances.

1. With right sides together, assemble the background as shown. Press each seam as you go. Sew F to the left side of the center A. Sew H to I and then sew H/I to A/F. Sew the 3″ × 3″ squares into a row (B, C, D, and E). Then sew this 4-square row to the left side of the A/F/H/I unit. Add G to the right side of this unit and J to the top to complete the background.

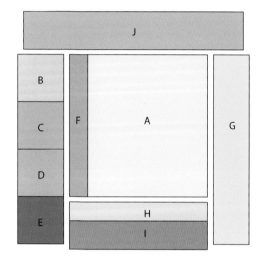

2. Iron fusible web to the wrong side of the elephant fabric, following the manufacturer's instructions. Cut out the elephant and fuse it in place on your block. Machine stitch the elephant in place using a zigzag or blanket stitch.

3. Cut notches in the seam allowance of the elephant ear appliqué for smooth curves. Pin the ear and needle-turn appliqué it in place.

4. Embroider the mouse on top of the elephant's ear using a backstitch with brown perle cotton.

5. Embroider the elephant's eye and feet in brown using a backstitch and satin stitch.

6. Stitch around the elephant's ear and body with a running stitch in perle cotton.

7. Stitch around the edge of the block center with a running stitch.

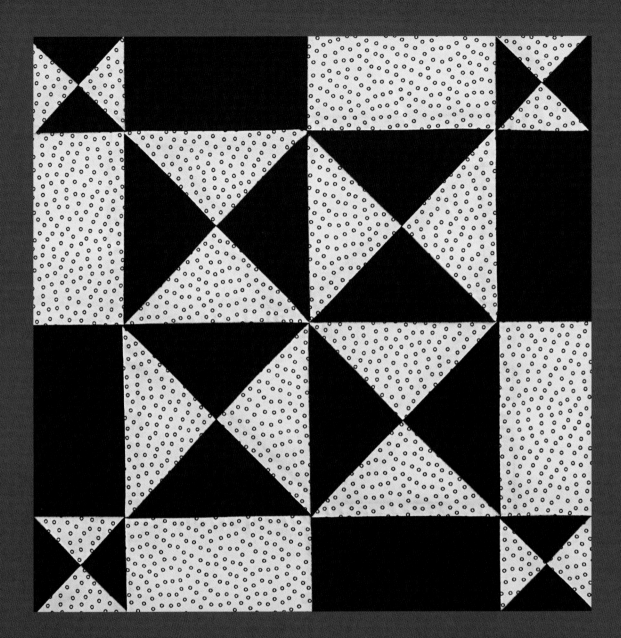

NIGHT AND **DAY**

designed by
Kimberly Walus

This 12″ × 12″ (finished) quilt block makes a great two-color quilt
because of the two highly contrasting colors—in this example, white and black.
Enjoy playing with different color combinations. There are lots of options
for this simple yet sophisticated-looking block.

SUPPLIES AND CUTTING

Light fabric

Cut 2 squares 3½" × 3½".

Cut 2 squares 5½" × 5½".

Cut 4 rectangles 2½" × 4½".

Dark fabric

Cut 2 squares 3½" × 3½".

Cut 2 squares 5½" × 5½".

Cut 4 rectangles 2½" × 4½".

Triangle square-up ruler by Eleanor Burns (*optional*)

HOW-TO

Use ¼" seam allowances.

1. Use a light 3½" × 3½" square and a dark 3½" × 3½" square to make 2 half-square triangle units (page 27). Press the seam allowance toward the dark fabric. Repeat to make 4 half-square triangle units.

2. With right sides together, match up 2 of the half-square triangles by placing the dark halves against the light halves and the light halves against the dark halves, with the seams meeting in the middle. Draw a diagonal line perpendicular to the sewn seams from one corner to the opposite corner.

3. Sew ¼" from each side of the drawn line. Cut on the drawn line.

4. Repeat Steps 2 and 3 with the remaining half-square triangles from Step 1.

5. Repeat Steps 1–4 using 2 light 5½" × 5½" squares and 2 dark 5½" × 5½" squares.

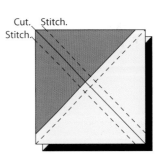

Place right sides together, aligning diagonal seams.

6. Square up the smaller quarter-square triangle units to 2½" × 2½" and the larger quarter-square triangle units to 4½" × 4½", making certain that the intersection of the seams stays in the middle of each unit.

7. Arrange all the quarter-square units and the 2½" × 4½" rectangles as shown. With right sides together, sew the units and rectangles into rows, pressing the seams in adjacent rows in opposite directions. Sew the rows together to complete the block.

designed by Weeks Ringle and Bill Kerr

ON THE **FENCE**

There is a confidence in using just two colors. When every other block is rotated 90 degrees, you'll get a striking variation of the traditional Rail Fence block. The narrow ¼″ strips of white contrast sharply with the richness of the red.

SUPPLIES AND CUTTING

Red fabric

Cut 2 strips 3¼" × 12½".

Cut 5 strips 1½" × 12½".

White fabric

Cut 6 strips ¾" × 12½".

HOW-TO

Use ¼" seam allowances.

1. With right sides together, sew a ¾" × 12½" white strip to the bottom of each 1½" × 12½" red strip. Sew the remaining ¾" × 12½" white strip to the bottom of a 3¼" × 12½" red strip. Press all the seams open.

2. Lay the strips out as shown in Step 1. With right sides together, sew the units together. Add a 3¼" × 12½" red strip to the bottom of the block. Press the seams open. Trim the block to 12½" × 12½".

designed by Emily Cier

ON THE **PLUS SIDE**

Today we blast ourselves back to the past and reenter first grade.
We will learn all about addition in today's lesson. It's like a big math
worksheet bundled up into one quilt block.

SUPPLIES AND CUTTING

Blue fabric

Cut 1 strip 1½″ × fabric width.

Subcut as follows:

7 squares 1½″ × 1½″ (A)

4 rectangles 3½″ × 1½″ (B)

Orange fabric

Cut 1 strip 1½″ × fabric width.

Subcut as follows:

8 squares 1½″ × 1½″ (A)

2 rectangles 3½″ × 1½″ (B)

2 rectangles 2½″ × 1½″ (C)

Purple fabric

Cut 1 strip 1½″ × fabric width.

Subcut as follows:

8 squares 1½″ × 1½″ (A)

4 rectangles 3½″ × 1½″ (B)

White fabric

Cut 1 strip 1½″ × fabric with.

Subcut as follows:

7 squares 1½″ × 1½″ (A)

4 rectangles 3½″ × 1½″ (B)

Gray fabric for background

Cut 3 strips 1½″ × fabric width.

Subcut as follows:

10 squares 1½″ × 1½″ (A)

2 rectangles 3½″x 1½″ (B)

5 rectangles 2½″ × 1½″ (C)

1 strip 9½″ × 1½″ (D)

2 strips 8½″ × 1½″ (E)

1 strip 7½″ × 1½″ (F)

2 strips 5½″ × 1½″ (G)

HOW-TO

Use ¼″ seam allowances.

1. With right sides together, sew a 1½″ × 1½″ blue A square to a 2½″ × 1½″ gray C rectangle. Add the 9½″ × 1½″ gray D strip to the right side to complete the first row. Press the seams to one side.

Row 1

2. With right sides together, sew a 3½″ × 1½″ blue B rectangle to a 1½″ × 1½″ orange A square. Add an 8½″ × 1½″ gray E strip to the right side of the B rectangle to complete the second row. Press the seams in the opposite direction from Row 1.

Row 2

3. Continue to sew each row as shown in the diagram until all rows are complete. Press the seams of each row in the opposite direction of the previous row.

4. Sew the rows together. Press the seams open. Trim the block to 12½″ × 12½″.

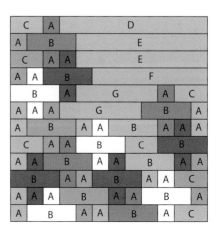

OPEN **BOOK**
designed by
Yvonne Malone

Experiment with the layout when using this block for an entire quilt. This block would look stunning in an asymmetrical layout. The books will almost appear to float when the quilt is viewed from a distance. Try laying out one vertical column of blocks set to the left of center or a single horizontal band two-thirds of the way down. Use the same background fabric as used for the blocks for the remainder of the quilt.

SUPPLIES AND CUTTING

Template patterns are on page 215.

Print fabric

Cut 1 using Template A.

Cut 1 using Template A reversed.

Red solid fabric

Cut 2 using Template B.

Cut 2 using Template B reversed.

Cut 1 strip 1″ × 9″.

Cut 2 strips 2¼″ × 9″.

Cut 2 strips 2¼″ × 12½″.

Template plastic

HOW-TO

Use ¼″ seam allowances.

1. With right sides together, sew the A's to the B's to form 2 pieced rectangles as shown. Press the seams open. Trim off any dog-ears.

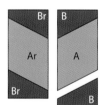

2. Arrange the pieces as shown. With right sides together, sew the block together as follows, pressing the seams open after each section is added: Sew a 1″ × 9″ red strip between the 2 rectangles from Step 1. Sew a 2¼″ × 9″ red strip to either side. Sew 2¼″ × 12½″ strips to the top and bottom of the block. Trim the block to 12½″ × 12½″.

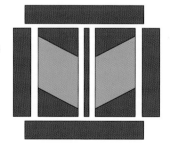

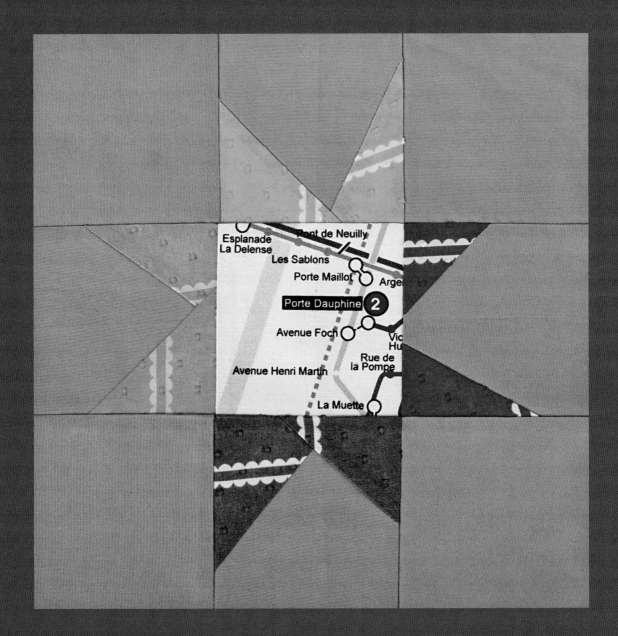

PARISIAN **STAR** designed by Leanne Cohen

No longer limited to calico, today's quilt designers are using voile, cotton lawn, linen, and a host of other types of fabrics. This wonky star is a great way to showcase all these different fabrics and textures.

SUPPLIES AND CUTTING

Linen print for center

Cut 1 square 4½" × 4½".

Solid gray fabric for background

Cut 8 squares 4½" × 4½".

Voile fabrics in 4 colors for star points*

Cut 1 square 4½" × 4½" from each color. Cut each square in half on the diagonal.

Line each fabric with sheer stabilizer before cutting when using lightweight fabrics such as voile.

HOW-TO

Use ¼" seam allowances.

1. With right sides together, place a star point triangle on the right side of a background square. Make sure the ends of the star point extend beyond the sides of the background square. Sew along the long edge of the triangle and trim any excess background fabric, leaving a ¼" seam allowance. Open the star point and press.

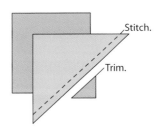

2. With right sides together, add a star point triangle to an adjacent corner of the gray square in the same color and fabric used in Step 1. Sew along the long edge of the triangle, trim the background, and press open. Trim the star point unit to 4½" × 4½".

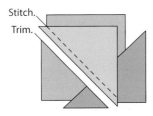

3. Repeat Steps 1 and 2 to make 4 star point units.

4. Arrange the center square, background squares, and star point units as shown in the block photo (page 128). With right sides together, sew the squares into rows and press the seams in adjacent rows in opposite directions. Sew the rows together, press, and trim to 12½" × 12½".

PATHWAYS

designed by
Weeks Ringle and Bill Kerr

This block can make it easy to coordinate a quilt with a room. Begin by selecting a single hue—in this case, blue. Then select four different values of that same color. Depending on how similar or different the values of the fabrics are, the block can read quite differently. For instance, if the center squares are significantly lighter, they may pop. If the three lighter blues are close in value but the field fabric is much darker, then you'll create a smoother blending of colors.

SUPPLIES AND CUTTING

Dark blue fabric

Cut 1 center square 4½″ × 4½″.

Cut 4 corner squares 2½″ × 2½″.

Cut 4 edge rectangles 2½″ × 4½″.

Lightest blue fabric

Cut 4 squares 2½″ × 2½″.

Medium-light blue fabric

Cut 16 rectangles 2½″ × 1½″.

Medium blue fabric

Cut 8 rectangles 2½″ × 1½″.

Cut 4 squares 2½″ × 2½″.

HOW-TO

Use ¼″ seam allowances.

1. With right sides together, sew a 2½″ × 1½″ medium blue rectangle to a 2½″ × 1½″ medium-light blue rectangle to create an A unit. Press the seams open. Make 8.

A unit—
Make 8.

2. With right sides together, sew a 2½″ × 1½″ medium-light blue rectangle to either side of a 2½″ × 2½″ medium blue square to make a B unit. Press the seams open. Make 4.

B unit—Make 4.

3. With right sides together, sew the A and B units and remaining pieces into 5 columns as shown. Press the seams open.

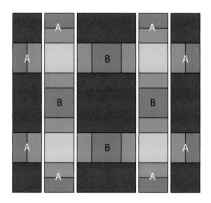

4. With right sides together, sew the columns together, pinning carefully to align the seams. Press the seams open.

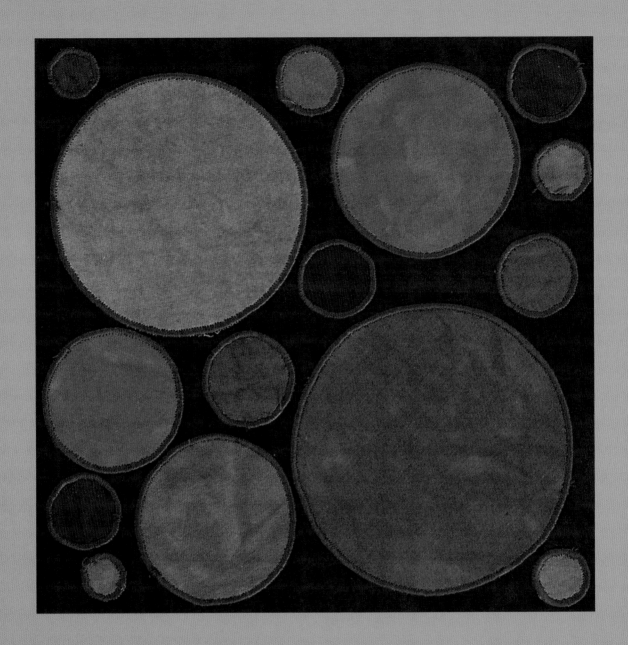

PEBBLE **BEACH** designed by Kim Schaefer

Choose earthy tones for subtlety or make a splash with bright circles
on a contrasting background.

SUPPLIES AND CUTTING

Blue fabric

Cut 1 square 13″ × 13″. Trim to 12½″ × 12½″ after appliqué.

Green fabric scraps for appliqué

Paper-backed fusible web

HOW-TO

Template patterns are on page 216.

1. Trace the circles as follows onto the paper side of the fusible web:

Trace 2 circles using Template A.

Trace 3 circles using Template B.

Trace 3 circles using Template C.

Trace 1 circle each using Templates D, E, F, G, H, I, and J.

2. Cut out the circles from the fusible web ¼″ outside the drawn lines.

3. Iron the cut-out circles of fusible web (following the manufacturer's instructions) onto the wrong side of the appliqué fabrics. Cut out the fabric circles on the drawn lines and peel off the backing paper.

4. Fuse the circles to the background fabric. Refer to the layout diagram for placement.

5. Stitch around the raw edges of the circles with a small zigzag stitch. Trim the block to 12½″ × 12½″.

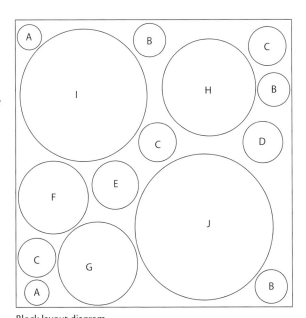

Block layout diagram

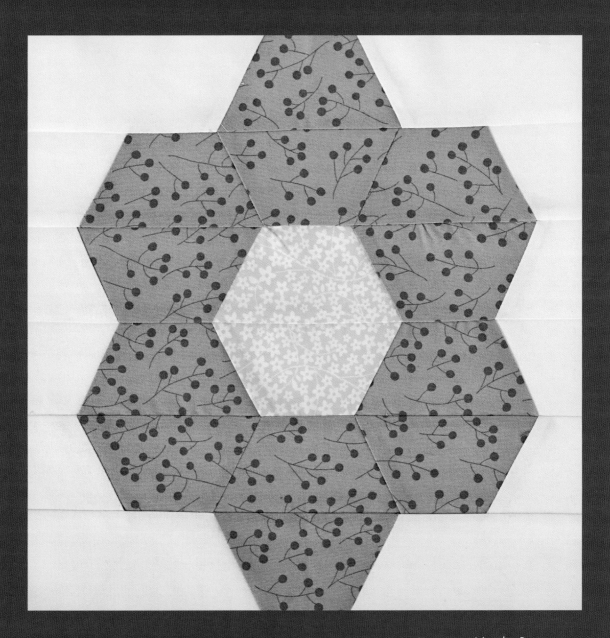

designed by Natalia Bonner

PIECE OF THE **GARDEN**

Just like a Grandmother's Flower Garden block, only bigger.
Create a bouquet of posies with this easy-to-piece block.

SUPPLIES AND CUTTING

Template patterns are on pages 216 and 217.

White fabric for background

Cut 2 using Template A.

Cut 2 using Template A reversed.

Cut 4 using Template B.

Cut 4 using Template B reversed.

Pink print fabric for flower

Cut 12 using Template C.

Yellow print fabric for flower center

Cut 2 using Template C.

HOW-TO

Use ¼" seam allowances.

1. Arrange the pieces as shown in the assembly diagram. With right sides together, sew the pieces together in rows. Press.

2. With right sides together, sew the rows together. Press

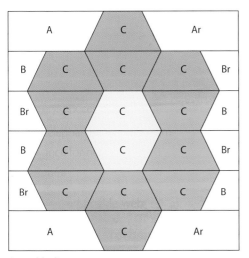

Assembly diagram

designed by Jessica Brown

PINBALL **MACHINE**

Constructed somewhat like a traditional Log Cabin block, the asymmetrical rings
of this variation create a lot of movement, especially with high-contrast fabrics.
An improv version would add even more visual interest. When using these blocks
in a quilt, try rotating some of the blocks 90 degrees when setting them. Or perhaps
make a couple of the rings out of another color or a complementary print.

SUPPLIES AND CUTTING

Green fabric

Cut 1 square 1½" × 1½" (A).

Cut 1 strip 3½" × 1¼" (F).

Cut 1 strip 1¼" × 4¼" (G).

Cut 1 strip 2¾" × 4¼" (H).

Cut 1 strip 6½" × 2¾" (I).

Cut 1 strip 9½" × 1¾" (N).

Cut 1 strip 1¾" × 10¾" (O).

Cut 1 strip 2¼" × 10¾" (P).

Cut 1 strip 12½" × 2¼" (Q).

Pale blue fabric

Cut 1 strip 1½" × 1" (B).

Cut 1 strip 1" × 2" (C).

Cut 1 square 2" × 2" (D).

Cut 1 strip 3½" × 2" (E).

Cut 1 strip 6½" × 1½" (J).

Cut 1 strip 1½" × 7½" (K).

Cut 1 strip 2½" × 7½" (L).

Cut 1 strip 9½" × 2½" (M).

HOW-TO

Use ¼" seam allowances and press the seams open as you piece.

1. Sew pale blue strip B to the bottom of green square A. Press. Sew blue strip C to the right side of this unit and blue square D to the left side. Press. Add blue strip E to the top of the unit and press. Square the unit to 3½" × 3½".

2. Make the next ring of the block: Add green strip F to the top, strip G to the left, and rectangle H to the right side. Finish by sewing rectangle I to the bottom. Press and then square to 6½" × 6½".

3. Add the next blue ring to the block: Stitch pale blue strip J to the bottom. Sew strip K to the right of the unit and strip L to the left. Finish the blue ring by sewing strip M to the top. Press and then square to 9½" × 9½".

4. Finish the block with the outermost ring: Sew green strip N to the top of the unit from Step 3. Sew green strip O to the left of the block and green strip P to the right side. Finish by sewing green strip Q to the bottom. Press and then square the block to 12½" × 12½".

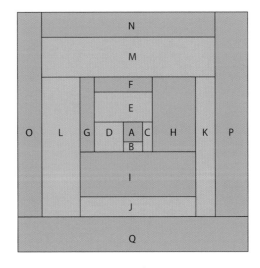

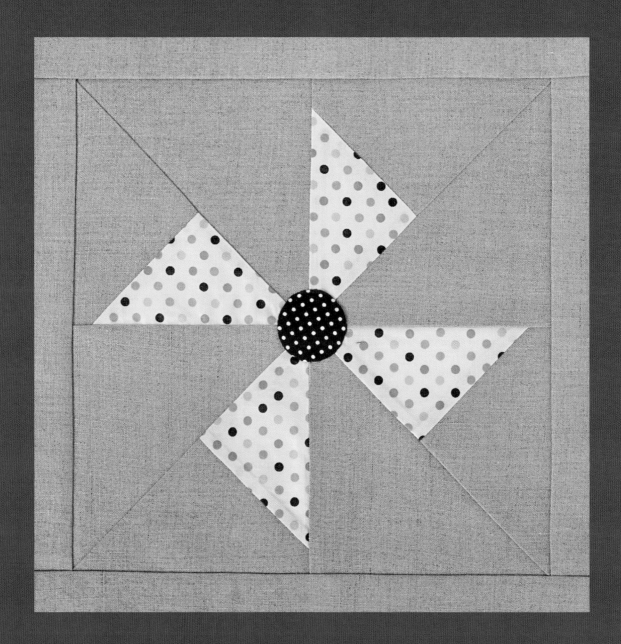

PINWHEEL designed by Amy Sinibaldi

Using a whole batch of these Pinwheel blocks to make a quilt
would be a delight because you could choose any number of coordinating or,
even better, mismatched prints to create a fun and colorful quilt.
Sash the blocks in white to make them really pop.

SUPPLIES AND CUTTING

Linen fabric

Cut 2 squares 5⅞″ × 5⅞″. Cut each square in half on the diagonal to make 4 A triangles.

Cut 2 squares 4⅞″ × 4⅞″. Cut each square in half on the diagonal to make 4 B triangles.

Cut 2 strips 1½″ × 10½″.

Cut 2 strips 12½″ × 1½″.

Cream polka dot fabric

Cut 2 squares 4⅛″ × 4⅛″. Cut each square in half on the diagonal to make 4 C triangles.

Red polka dot fabric

Cut 1 circle 2″ in diameter using the template pattern (page 219).

HOW-TO

Use ¼″ seam allowances.

1. Sew a linen B triangle to a polka dot C triangle, joining 2 short sides. Trim the corner of the B triangle as shown. Make 4.

2. Sew an A triangle to the B/C unit from Step 1, joining the long sides of the triangles. Press. Trim the unit to 5½″ × 5½″. Make 4.

3. Using the block photo (page 138) as a guide, arrange 4 squares from Step 2 and sew as a four-patch.

4. Sew 1½″ × 10½″ linen strips to the left and right sides of the block and press.

5. Sew 12½″ × 1½″ linen strips to the top and bottom of the block and press.

6. Pin and neddle-turn appliqué the red circle to the center of the block.

7. Trim the block to 12½″ × 12½″.

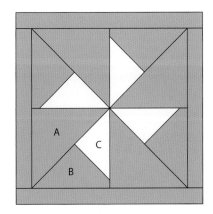

PIXEL **PEAKS** designed by Amy Ellis

This block creates a bold effect. If you are making a quilt with this block, consider having all the peaks face one direction. Or have them face opposite directions to make a diamond shape. Using a bold color as the main color makes a dramatic statement—and the color can be chosen to match any decor!

SUPPLIES AND CUTTING

¼ yard or 1 fat quarter (18″ × 22″) red fabric

Cut 3 strips 2″ × fabric width. (If using a fat quarter, cut 6 strips 2″ × 22″.) Subcut into:

> 2 rectangles 2″ × 12½″ (A)
>
> 2 rectangles 2″ × 6″ (B)
>
> 2 rectangles 2″ × 5″ (C)
>
> 2 rectangles 2″ × 4″ (D)
>
> 2 rectangles 2″ × 3″ (E)
>
> 2 squares 2″ × 2″ (F)
>
> 2 rectangles 2″ × 1″ (G)
>
> 1 rectangle 2″ × 1½″ (H)
>
> 1 rectangle 2″ × 3½″ (I)
>
> 1 rectangle 2″ × 5½″ (J)
>
> 1 rectangle 2″ × 7½″ (K)
>
> 1 rectangle 2″ × 9½″ (L)

Cream fabric

Cut 11 rectangles 1½″ × 2″ (H).

HOW-TO

1. Arrange the pieces as shown.

2. Working from left to right, with right sides together, sew the pieces together to create rows. Press toward the darker fabric.

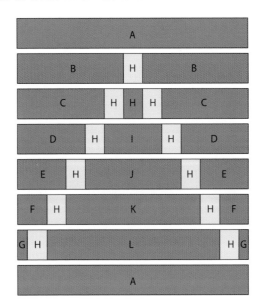

3. With right sides together, sew the rows together, carefully matching the seams as needed.

4. Press the seams in one direction.

5. Trim the block to 12½″ × 12½″.

POGO **STICK** designed by Jessica Brown

This simple modular block results in a complex final quilt. Alternating the direction of the blocks when setting them creates a woven effect. For a really colorful quilt, try a different color in place of some of the green center pieces. Or add a third color to replace the teal for the center strip and opposing end strips.

SUPPLIES AND CUTTING

Green fabric

Cut 1 strip 4½" × 5½" (A).

Cut 2 strips 2½" × 7½" (B).

Cut 2 strips 5" × 5¾" (C).

Teal fabric

Cut 2 strips 2" × 4½" (D).

Cut 2 strips 2" × 8½" (E).

Cut 1 strip 2" × 5" (F).

Cut 1 strip 2" × 12½" (G).

HOW-TO

Use ¼" seam allowances and press the seams open as you piece.

1. With right sides together, sew a teal strip D to the top and bottom of the green strip A. Press.

2. With right sides together, sew a teal strip E to each side of the unit from Step 1. Press.

3. With right sides together, sew a green strip B to the top and bottom of the unit from Step 2 as shown. Press. Set aside.

4. With right sides together, sew a green strip C to the top and bottom of the teal strip F. Press. Cut the unit in half as shown, creating 2 pieces 2½" × 12½".

5. With right sides together, sew a 2½" × 12½" unit from Step 5 to either side of the 7½" × 12½" unit from Step 3 as shown. Press. Cut the unit in half vertically to create 2 pieces 5¾" × 12½".

6. With right sides together, insert a teal strip G as shown. Press and then square the block to 12½" × 12½".

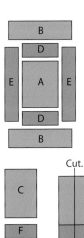

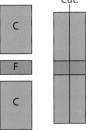

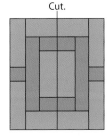

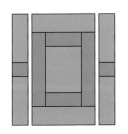

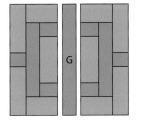

POLAROID
designed by
Susanne Woods

Use Transfer Artist Paper (TAP) or a similar product to transfer your photographs onto fabric. Cut to look like it includes one of the iconic instant camera photographs, this block would make a quick and easy memory quilt with a modern twist.

SUPPLIES AND CUTTING

White fabric (at least 6″ × 6″)

Transfer image onto white fabric before cutting.

Cut 1 square 6″ × 6″.

Black fabric

Cut 2 rectangles 3¾″ × 6″.

Cut 2 rectangles 3¾″ × 12½″.

Brown print fabric

Cut 4 squares 3″ × 3″.

HOW-TO

Use ¼″ seam allowances.

1. Transfer a 3½″ × 5″ image onto a piece of white fabric at least 6″ × 6″. Trim the fabric to 6″ × 6″, centering the photo image so that there is a ½″ strip of white on the top and sides of the image and a wider white strip on the bottom.

2. With right sides together, sew the 6″ × 3¾″ black rectangles to the top and bottom of the white fabric. Press. With right sides together, sew the 3¾″ × 12½″ black rectangles to the left and right sides of the white fabric. Press.

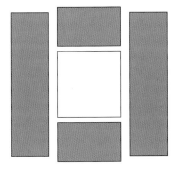

3. On the wrong side of each 3″ × 3″ brown print square, use a pencil and ruler to draw a diagonal line from one corner to the other.

4. With right sides together, pin and sew the print squares to the corners of the blocks. Stitch along the pencil lines on the backs of the 3″ × 3″ squares. Trim the excess fabric ¼″ away from the stitch line. Press open.

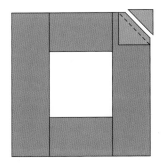

POTAGER designed by
Yvonne Malone

This block is based on the half-square triangle, a traditional unit used in Pinwheel block quilts and other classic designs. I love the half-square triangle for its versatility. It can take on many different looks depending on the fabrics selected.

SUPPLIES AND CUTTING

Medium orange print fabric

Cut 2 squares 6″ × 6″. Then cut in half on the diagonal.

Off-white tone-on-tone fabric

Cut 2 squares 6⅝″ × 6⅝″. Then cut in half on the diagonal.

Cut 2 strips 1″ × 6¼″.

Cut 1 strip 1″ × 12½″.

Dark orange tone-on-tone fabric

Cut 4 strips 1″ × 10½″.

Spray starch (*optional*)

TIP Lightly spray the dark orange fabric with starch before cutting the required number of pieces to help the strips hold their shape during sewing.

HOW-TO

Use ¼″ seam allowances. Press the seams open.

1. With right sides together, sew a dark orange strip to each medium orange print triangle, centering the strip on the long (8½″) edge of the triangle. Repeat to form 4 triangles.

2. Trim each dark orange strip so that the ends are even with the triangle.

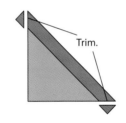

Trim.

3. With right sides together, sew a pieced triangle to each off-white triangle along the long edges. Trim off the dog-ears. Repeat to form 4 squares. Press. Each completed square should measure 6¼″ × 6¼″.

4. Arrange the pieced squares and white strips as shown. With right sides together, sew the block together and press. Trim the block to 12½″ × 12½″.

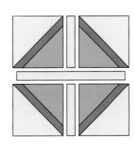

designed by Laura West Kong

QUARTER-CUT **DAISY**

This block is inspired by the traditional New York Beauty block. Large fusible appliqué pieces make it quick and easy. The background square and flower center are perfect for showing off funky large-scale modern prints. Use tone-on-tone prints or hand-dyed fabrics for the arc and flower petals. Make a bunch of blocks and have fun trying out all the different New York Beauty settings.

SUPPLIES AND CUTTING

Background fabric

Cut 1 square 12½″ × 12½″.

Arc fabric

Cut 1 square 11¼″ × 11¼″.

Petal fabric

Cut 1 rectangle 7″ × 13″.

Flower center fabric

Cut 1 square 7″ × 7″.

Paper-backed fusible web

Cut 1 square 17″ × 17″.

HOW-TO

Template patterns are on page 217. Enlarge by 200%.

1. Trace the lines of the enlarged pattern pieces onto the paper side of the fusible web. Cut out the fusible web pieces, leaving a margin of at least ¼″ around each piece.

> **TIP** If desired, cut out the center of the fusible web pieces to make the finished block softer. Leave a margin of approximately ½″. If the fabric underneath is darker, cutting out the center of the fusible web also allows you to cut away the excess fabric underneath after you have fused the pieces down, so it will not show through.

2. Iron the cut-out fusible web pieces onto the wrong side of the appropriate fabric, following the manufacturer's instructions. Cut out the fused fabric pieces on the traced lines (including the overlap on the arc).

3. Using the block photo (page 148) and the edges of the 12½″ × 12½″ background square as a placement guide, fuse the arc to the background, following the manufacturer's instructions.

4. Place and fuse the A (3), B, and B reversed petals. Then place and fuse the flower center.

5. Use a narrow zigzag stitch and coordinating thread to cover the raw edges of the appliqué pieces. If desired, trim the excess fabric from behind the appliqués.

QUATREFOIL
designed by
Solidia Hubbard

e word *quatrefoil* means a flower with four petals or leaves. This block has quickly

become one of my favorites. For a quilt, you could make the centers all the same

r put a fussy-cut square in the center. Varying the background color to a gray or a

ocolate brown would be pretty. Or how about a quilt made in all feed-sack prints?

SUPPLIES AND CUTTING

White fabric

Cut 2 strips 2½" × 10".

Cut 8 squares 2½" × 2½".

Red fabric

Cut 1 strip 2½" × 10".

Red multiprint fabric

Cut 1 strip 2½" × 10".

Green floral fabric

Cut 4 squares 4½" × 4½".

Ruler print fabric for center

Cut 1 square 4½" × 4½".

HOW-TO

Use ¼" seam allowances.

1. With right sides together, sew a 2½" × 10" white strip to a 2½" × 10" red strip along the long sides. Press toward the red. Crosscut into 4 rectangles 2½" wide.

2. Repeat Step 1 with the white and red multiprint strips.

3. Pair a red/white rectangle with a red multiprint / white rectangle to make a four-patch. Make 4.

4. Draw a diagonal line on the wrong side of each 2½" × 2½" white square. With right sides together, place a white square in the corner of a 4½" × 4½" green floral square and sew along the drawn line. Trim the excess green floral fabric ¼" from the stitch line and press open. Repeat in an adjacent corner. Make 4.

5. With right sides together, sew the units into 3 rows as shown. Press. Sew the rows together. Press.

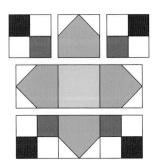

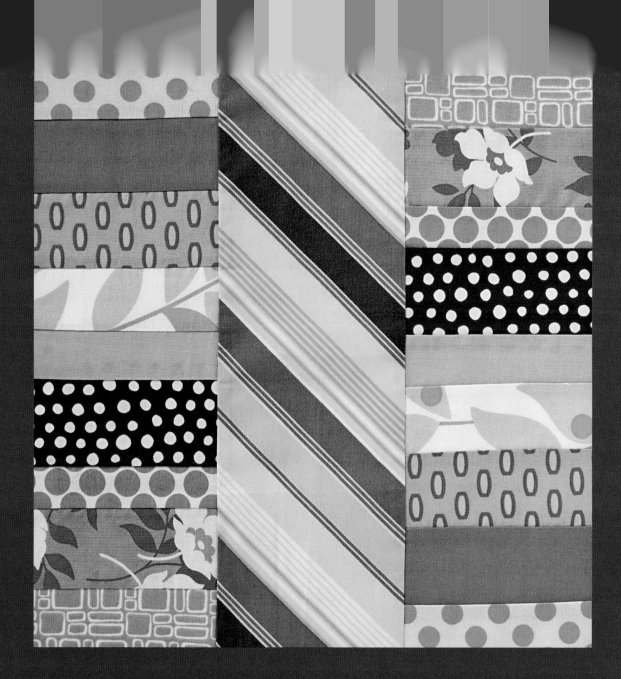

RIVERBANK
designed by
Tiffany Stephens

This easy-to-make block uses strips of fabric in varying sizes, so you can pull
from your scrap bag. Strips are sewn together, cut in half, and then flipped
on either side of the focus fabric. This block would also look great
with coordinating fabrics for a less scrappy look.

SUPPLIES AND CUTTING

Focus fabric

Cut 1 rectangle 4½" × 12½".

Assorted print fabrics

Cut 10–12 strips 9" long and varying in width from 1½" to 2½".

HOW-TO

Use ¼" seam allowances.

1. With right sides together, sew the assorted print strips together. Press and trim to measure 9" × 12½". Cut the rectangle vertically into 2 rectangles 4½" × 12½" each.

2. With right sides together, sew a pieced rectangle from Step 1 to the left side of the 4½" × 12½" focus fabric rectangle. Rotate the remaining pieced strip and sew it to the right side of the focus fabric. Press and trim the block to 12½" × 12½".

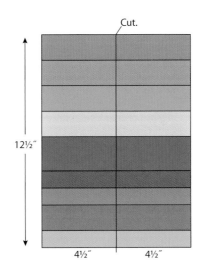

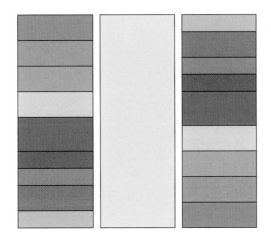

ROLLING **HILLS**
designed by
Krista Fleckenstein

The Rolling Hills block features gentle curves and is cut using a simple technique that creates two blocks instead of one. Just stack your rectangles of fabric, make a single curved cut, and you're ready to piece. Experiment with multiple variations of the block to create gentle waves.

SUPPLIES AND CUTTING

Before cutting, iron the fabric and use spray starch to stabilize it.

Green fabric

Cut 1 rectangle 12½" × 13".

Blue fabric

Cut 1 rectangle 12½" × 13".

Water-soluble marker or tailor's chalk

HOW-TO

Use ¼" seam allowances.

1. Trace the block outline and curve shape from the block photo (page 154) and enlarge by 200%.

2. With both fabrics right side up, place the green fabric rectangle on top of the blue rectangle, aligning all the edges.

3. Center a template made from the enlarged block photo and trace the curved line onto the top piece of fabric, using a water-soluble marker or tailor's chalk.

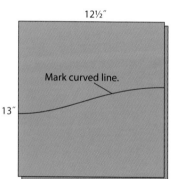

12½"

Mark curved line.

13"

4. Cut the curved line with a rotary cutter, making certain to cut through both pieces of fabric. When you are done, you will have 2 pieces of blue fabric and 2 pieces of green fabric. Shuffle the layers so that you have the layout for 2 blocks, each with a green and a blue piece that fit together like the block photo.

5. With right sides facing, pin the pieces together, placing pins every ½". Stitch. Press the seam allowance toward the darker fabric.

TIPS

· When using only solids, you can use the "wrong side" of the fabrics after they are cut to create a block that is the mirror image of the one shown. When alternating blocks are sewn together in a row, a rolling hills pattern will emerge.

· When using printed fabrics, trace the template onto the wrong side of the fabric to create a block that is the mirror image of the one shown.

designed by **Sonja Callaghan**

RUSSELL THE **ROBOT**

I don't know why, but I just love creating cute and quirky paper-pieced quilt patterns for boys. Russell the Robot is a wonderfully versatile block with virtually endless color combinations. Just make sure that Russell is easy to see against the background. Have fun—before you know it, you'll have sewn up all sorts of buddies for Russell!

SUPPLIES AND CUTTING

Dark blue fabric

Cut 1 square 6″ × 6″ for the arms.

Light blue fabric

Cut 1 square 6″ × 6″ for the shoulders.

Red fabric

Cut 1 square 6″ × 6″ for the head.

Yellow fabric

Cut 1 square 6″ × 6″ for the chest.

Light gray fabric

Cut 1 square 6″ × 6″ for the legs.

White fabric

Cut 1 square 20″ × 20″ for the face and background foundation piecing.

Cut 1 rectangle 4½″ × 12½″ for the background (section A).

Dark gray fabric

Cut 1 square 12″ × 12″ for the elbows, torso, and feet.

Green fabric

Cut 1 rectangle 2″ × 12½″ for the ground (section N).

Foundation paper, such as Simple Foundations Translucent Vellum Paper or Carol Doak's Foundation Paper

HOW-TO

Enlarge the paper-piecing patterns (page 218) by 200% before using them.

> **TIP** If you are not familiar with paper piecing, try one of the following resources:
>
> · *Every Quilter's Foundation Piecing Reference Tool* by Jane Hall and Dixie Haywood
>
> · *Carol Doak Teaches You to Paper Piece* DVD

1. Trace the enlarged patterns onto foundation paper and divide into lettered sections.

2. Working with one section at a time, piece the appropriate fabrics onto the foundation. Trim the edges, leaving a ¼″ seam allowance on all sides of each section. Press as you sew. Leave the foundation paper in place until the entire block is pieced and trimmed.

3. With right sides together, sew the sections together as follows, using the edges of the foundation paper as a guide. Assemble the left arm by joining sections B, C, D, and E. Assemble the body by joining sections F, G, H, and I. Assemble the right arm by joining sections J, K, L, and M.

4. Sew the arm sections to the left and right sides of the body. Add section A to the top of the assembled sections. Add section N to the bottom of the assembled sections.

5. Press thoroughly, trim the outer edges of the block ¼″ beyond the foundation paper, and remove the foundation paper.

RUSSELL THE ROBOT

SATURN'S **RINGS** designed by Latifah Saafir

This block uses bias strip appliqué. When fabric is cut along the bias (at a 45-degree angle to the selvage), it provides enough give that it can easily create curved shapes. The bias strips are pinned in place and then topstitched down to make a simple, graphic quilt block. The quarter-circle curves in this block are not designed to be exact; they are designed to be organic and a bit wonky.

SUPPLIES AND CUTTING

Aqua fabric

Cut 1 strip on the bias 2″ × 21″.

Teal fabric

Cut 1 strip on the bias 2″ × 18″.

Red fabric

Cut 1 strip on the bias 2″ × 15″.

Light aqua fabric

Cut 1 strip on the bias 2″ × 11″.

Light gray fabric for background

Cut 1 square 12½″ × 12½″.

1″ bias tape maker (*optional*)

HOW-TO

1. Make 1″-wide bias folded strips from the aqua, turquoise, red, and light aqua pieces by pressing under each long edge ½″.

2. Using the block photo (page 158) as a guide, position the outer aqua bias strip on the background fabric and pin it in place. *Note: There should be a bit of extra length to give you a little freedom in placement.* Pin the remaining bias strips in place, about 1″ apart.

3. Using a straight stitch, carefully topstitch the top edges of the bias strips, removing the straight pins as you sew. Repeat along the bottom edges.

4. Trim the ends of the bias strips to make the block 12½″ × 12½″.

designed by **Louise Papas**

SEA GLASS **STEPS**

Reminiscent of the ocean, these beautiful sea greens and blues will make you feel like you are on vacation! This block was designed so that the main center and border color alternate from blue to green. You can also play around with the layout: Run the blocks so that they all go diagonally to the left or right quilt corner or alternate them to create a lovely zigzag effect.

SUPPLIES AND CUTTING

Blue-green fabric

Cut 2 strips 2½" × 12½".

Cut 2 strips 2½" × 8½".

Cut 1 square 2½" × 2½".

Cut 2 squares 1½" × 1½".

Green fabric

Cut 4 squares 1½" × 1½".

White fabric

Cut 2 rectangles 3½" × 5½".

Cut 2 rectangles 2½" × 3½".

Cut 4 strips 1½" × 2½".

Cut 4 squares 1½" × 1½".

HOW-TO

Use ¼" seam allowances.

1. With right sides together, assemble a four-patch unit as shown using 4 squares 1½" × 1½". Press. Make 2 units.

2. Add a white 1½" × 2½" strip to the right side of the four-patch unit from Step 1.

3. Sew a green 1½" × 1½" square to a white 1½" × 2½" strip. Attach this unit to the bottom of the unit from Step 2 as shown. Repeat Steps 1–3 to make 2.

4. Add a 3½" × 5½" white rectangle to the bottom of each unit from Step 3. Press. Set aside.

5. Sew a 2½" × 3½" white rectangle to either side of the 2½" × 2½" blue-green square. Press.

6. Arrange the units from Steps 4 and 5 into 3 vertical rows as shown. With right sides together, sew the rows together. Press

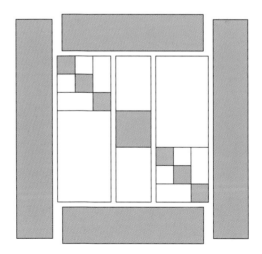

7. With right sides together, sew the 2½" × 8½" borders to the top and bottom of the center. Press. Sew the 2½" × 12½" side borders to the center. Press. Trim the block to 12½" × 12½".

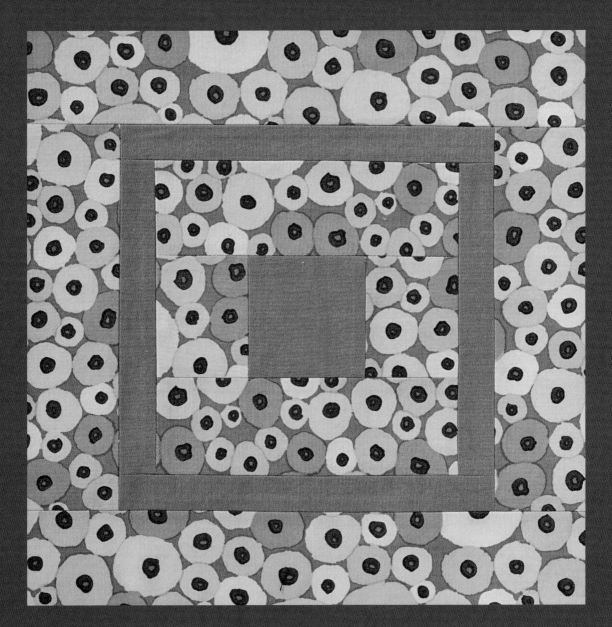

SEEING **DOUBLE** designed by Yvonne Malone

This simple block for all experience levels is all about color and is great for using small pieces of a favorite medium- to large-scale print. Although the fabric's design element (big flowers) will be lost when the pieces that make up this block are cut, the colors that made you fall in love with the fabric will still be there. This block works beautifully whether as a single square to put under a vase of flowers on a table or as part of a queen-size bed quilt.

SUPPLIES AND CUTTING

Lightly starch the fabrics to stabilize them while cutting and sewing.

Green print fabric

Cut 2 rectangles 2½″ × 3″ (B).

Cut 2 strips 2½″ × 7″ (C).

Cut 2 strips 2½″ × 8½″ (F).

Cut 2 strips 2½″ × 12½″ (G).

Gold solid fabric

Cut 1 square 3″ × 3″ (A).

Cut 2 strips 1¼″ × 7″ (D).

Cut 2 strips 1¼″ × 8½″ (E).

Spray starch (*optional*)

HOW-TO

Use ¼″ seam allowances. Press each seam open.

With right sides together, sew the pieces together in alphabetical order as shown.

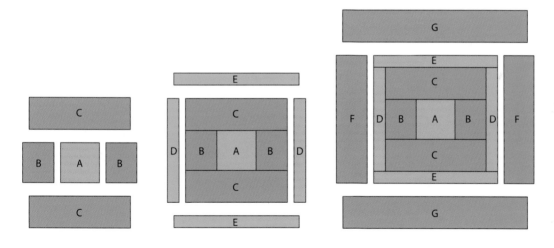

designed by Bari J. Ackerman

SELVAGE **STRINGS**

A string block is a traditional block. This foundation-pieced block is perfect
for using up the bits and scraps, or "strings," left over from other projects. I made this
one modern by using bright colors, varying the width of the "strings," and adding
little bits of selvage from the fabrics. The white that frames the center square was
created by leaving the center of the foundation free of strips.

SUPPLIES AND CUTTING

White fabric for foundations

Cut 4 squares 6½″ × 6½″.

Scraps for strings

Cut 20 strips in widths ranging from 1″ to 2″.

Erasable fabric pen or chalk

HOW-TO

Use ¼″ seam allowances.

Create 4 blocks 6½″ × 6½″:

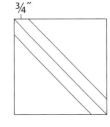

1. Using an erasable fabric pen or erasable chalk (check the fabric first to see if it will indeed erase), mark the center of each 6½″ × 6½″ square on the diagonal from corner to corner. Mark additional lines ¾″ to each side of the center line.

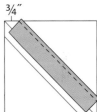

2. Line the raw edge of a strip right side down along one of the lines to the left or right of the center. Using a ¼″ seam allowance, stitch the strip to the white base fabric.

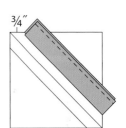

3. Flip the strip to the right side and press. Align a second strip on the right edge of the first strip, right sides together. Using a ¼″ seam allowance, stitch the second strip to the first strip.

4. Flip the second strip to the right side and press.

5. Repeat Steps 3 and 4 until you have covered half of the square.

6. Repeat Steps 2–5 for the other half of the square, leaving the center of the foundation exposed.

7. Trim the excess fabric around the square so it is 6½″ × 6½″.

8. Repeat Steps 1–7 to make 4 units.

9. Referring to the block photo (page 164), sew the 4 units together to finish the block. Press and trim to 12½″ × 12½″.

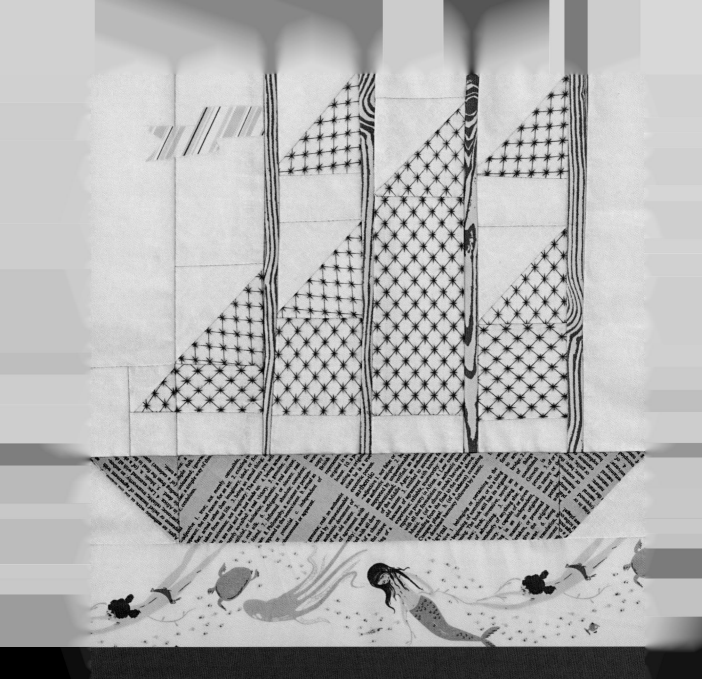

SET **SAIL** designed by Susanne Woods

Have fun choosing a fabric for the ocean strip on the bottom to tell your own story.
This is simple to piece, as most of the units are made from half-square triangles.
Embroider a name on the flag for a personalized touch.

SUPPLIES AND CUTTING

The flag template can be found on page 218.

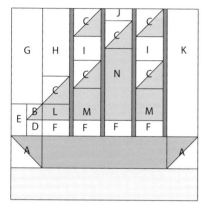

HOW-TO

Use ¼" seam allowances. Press each seam.

Mermaid fabric for water

Cut 1 strip 12½" × 2½".

Newsprint fabric for boat

Cut 1 square 2⅞" × 2⅞" (A).

Cut 1 strip 8½" × 2½".

Wood-grain fabric for masts

Cut 4 strips ¾" × 8½".

Cream fabric for sky

Cut 1 square 2⅞" × 2⅞" (A).

Cut 1 square 1⅞" × 1⅞" (B).

Cut 3 squares 2⅝" × 2⅝" (C).

Cut 1 square 1½" × 1½" (D).

Cut 1 strip 1½" × 2½" (E).

Cut 4 strips 2¼" × 1½" (F).

Cut 1 rectangle 2½" × 6½" (G).

Cut 1 rectangle 2¼" × 4¾" (H).

Cut 2 rectangles 2¼" × 2" (I).

Cut 1 rectangle 2¼" × 1¼" (J).

Cut 1 rectangle 2½" × 8½" (K).

Print fabric for sail

Cut 1 square 1⅞" × 1⅞" (B).

Cut 3 squares 2⅝" × 2⅝" (C).

Cut 1 rectangle 2¼" × 1½" (L).

Cut 2 rectangles 2¼" × 2½" (M).

Cut 1 rectangle 2¼" × 5" (N).

Scrap of striped fabric for flag

Small piece of fusible web

1. Pair the 2⅞" × 2⅞" newsprint square A with the 2⅞" × 2⅞" cream square A to make 2 half-square triangles (see Half-Square Triangle Units, page 27). Sew a half-square triangle A to either end of the 8½" × 2½" newsprint strip as shown. Press.

2. Pair a 1⅞" × 1⅞" cream square B with a 1⅞" × 1⅞" sail square B to make 2 half-square triangles. Discard a half-square triangle or use it in another Set Sail block. Sew a 1½" × 1½" cream square to the bottom of the remaining half-square triangle B. Add a 1½" × 2½" cream strip to the left as shown. Press.

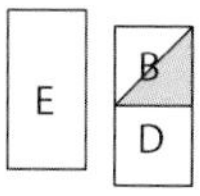

3. Pair a 2⅝" × 2⅝" cream square C with a 2⅝" × 2⅝" sail square C to make 2 half-square triangles. Repeat to make a total of 6 half-square triangles C. Press.

4. Arrange the units from Steps 2 and 3 with rectangles D–N as shown. With right sides together, sew into vertical rows. Press. Add ¾" × 8½" wood-grain strips to the right sides of the 4 center vertical rows. Press. Sew the vertical rows together and add a strip K to the right side to complete the top portion of the block. Press.

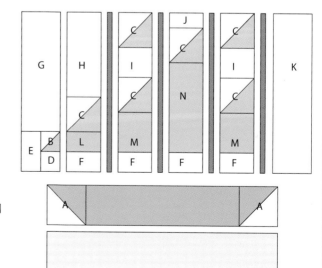

– – – – – Continued on page 206 – – – – –

SIMPLE **CIRCLE** designed by Cheryl Arkison

The circle fascination comes and goes for me. Discovering new fabric combinations, like the softer ones in this block, revived my circle love. Instead of the bright, high-contrast look I generally go for, this block uses what are sometimes referred to as low-volume fabrics—that is, predominantly white or neutral fabrics but with a graphic element. All together, these prints give a dynamic but softer quilt.

SUPPLIES AND CUTTING

Background fabric

Cut 1 square 12½″ × 12½″.

Circle fabric

Cut 1 square 10″ × 10″.

Freezer paper, 10″ × 10″

HOW-TO

1. Using a compass or a plate or bowl, draw a circle approximately 8½″ in diameter on the dull side of the freezer paper. Cut out the circle on the drawn line. Fold the freezer paper in quarters to find the center point.

2. Place the shiny side of the freezer paper on the wrong side of the fabric. Press to adhere the freezer paper to the fabric. Cut out the fabric circle about ½″ beyond the freezer paper. Don't remove the freezer paper. Make small marks in the seam allowance to mark the quarter-circles where the freezer paper folds fall.

3. By hand or using a long stitch on your sewing machine, baste ¼″ from the edge of the circle. Do not backstitch or stitch over your starting point. Leave long threads.

4. Holding the fabric circle and freezer paper on a firm surface, gently pull the long basting threads to gather the edges of the circle fabric over the freezer paper. Make sure all the edges are gathered and the circle lies flat. Press well to hold the gathered edge. Remove the freezer paper and press the circle again.

5. Fold the background square in quarters and press.

6. Center the fabric circle on the background fabric, lining up the quarter marks of the circle and the background square.

7. Appliqué the circle to the background square by hand or machine. Do not use a satin stitch.

8. Carefully trim away the background fabric from behind the circle. Press the block.

SLICE OF **HEAVEN** designed by Pat Sloan

I love the moon and stars image.
It looks fabulous when alternated with a pieced block.

SUPPLIES AND CUTTING

Blue fabric for background

Cut 1 square 12½″ × 12½″.

White fabric for moon

Cut 1 square 9″ × 9″.

Light yellow fabric for stars

Cut 1 rectangle 6″ × 13″.

Paper-backed fusible web

> **TIP** If you are using a light appliqué fabric on a dark background, check to see whether the dark fabric shows through. If it does, layer two appliqué shapes; the background shouldn't show through.

HOW-TO

1. Trace the appliqué shapes from the block photo (page 170) and enlarge the drawing by 200%.

2. Reverse the shapes and trace them onto the paper side of the fusible web. Cut them out ¼″ outside the drawn lines.

3. Iron the cut-out shapes of fusible web (following the manufacturer's instructions) onto the wrong side of the appliqué fabric. Cut out the fabric pieces on the drawn lines and peel off the backing paper.

4. Arrange and fuse the appliqué pieces onto the background square. Stitch around the shapes with a blanket stitch or a zigzag stitch.

SLOT **MACHINE** designed by Angela Pingel

This paper-pieced block is striking, with the sharp contrasts between the triangles, forming beautiful, crisp diamonds. It is equally lovely when made in a variety of prints and solids. A little tip: The prints help hide any less-than-perfect points. This block would be perfect at the ends of a table runner.

SUPPLIES AND CUTTING

Solid white fabric for foundation piecing, 30″ × 5″

Solid black fabric for foundation piecing, 20″ × 5″

Light gray fabric, 18″ × 5″

Cut 1 rectangle 2½″ × 4½″ (A).

Use the remaining fabric for foundation piecing.

Dark gray fabric, 18″ × 5″

Cut 1 rectangle 2½″ × 4½″ (B).

Use the remaining fabric for foundation piecing.

Foundation paper, such as Simple Foundations Translucent Vellum Paper or Carol Doak's Foundation Paper

TIP If you are not familiar with paper piecing, try one of the following resources:

· *Every Quilter's Foundation Piecing Reference Tool* by Jane Hall and Dixie Haywood

· *Carol Doak Teaches You to Paper Piece* DVD

HOW-TO

Use ¼″ seam allowances. The foundation pattern is on page 219.

1. Use your favorite paper-piecing technique to create each square unit. Assemble the unit by adding the pieces in numerical order from 1 to 4, using the block photo (page 172) to determine color placement. Be certain to leave a ¼″ seam allowance on all sides of the completed square unit. Make 8 square units.

Make 8.

2. With right sides together, sew the 2½″ × 4½″ light gray strip A to the top left pieced square unit. Do the same for the 2½″ × 4½″ dark gray strip B and the top right square unit. Press the seams away from the pieced squares and toward the solid gray strips.

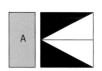

3. Sew the 2 units from Step 2 together, carefully matching the seam intersections to complete the top row. Press the seam open.

4. Assemble each of the remaining 3 diamonds by sewing 2 square units together, carefully matching the seam intersections and aligning the points of the diamonds. Press the seams open.

5. Sew the 3 vertical diamonds from Step 4 together, carefully matching the seam intersections and aligning the points of the diamonds. Press the seams open.

6. Sew the top row to the 3 vertical diamonds, carefully matching the seam intersections and aligning the points of the diamonds. Press the seams open. Trim to 12½″ × 12½″.

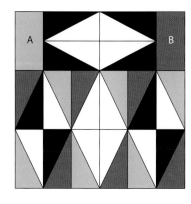

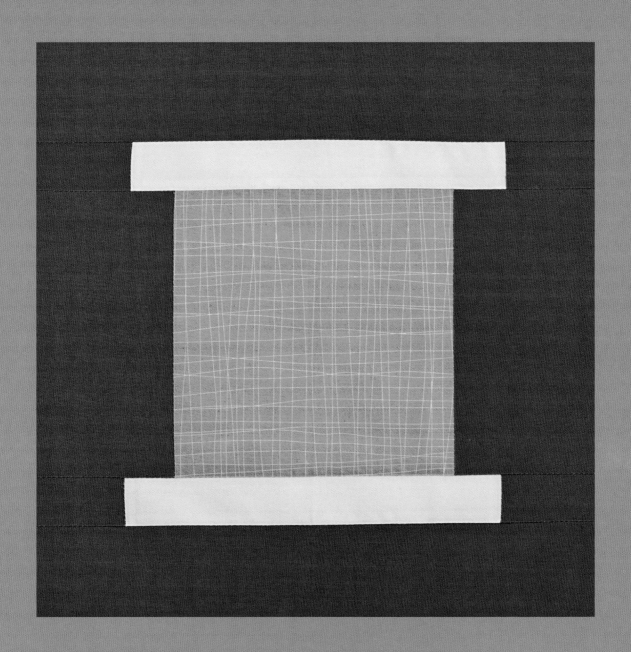

SPOOL designed by Krista Fleckenstein

What would a quilter do without the perfect spool of thread?
This modern Spool block is an updated version of the more traditional spool pattern
and is perfect for beginning quilters. This block is also great for showing off
a large-scale print in the thread area. Use solids in the background for high contrast.

SUPPLIES AND CUTTING

Yellow fabric

Cut 1 square 6½" × 6½" (A).

White fabric

Cut 2 strips 1½" × 8½" (C).

Gray fabric

Cut 2 strips 3½" × 6½" (B).

Cut 4 strips 1½" × 2½" (D).

Cut 2 strips 2½" × 12½" (E).

HOW-TO

Use ¼" seam allowances.

1. With right sides together, sew gray B strips to the left and right sides of the yellow A square. Press the seams open.

2. With right sides together, sew a gray D strip to either end of each white C strip. Press the seams open.

3. With right sides together, sew the white and gray pieced strips to the top and bottom of the yellow and gray pieced strip from Step 1. Press the seams open.

4. With right sides together, sew the gray E strips to the top and bottom of the block. Press the seams open. Trim the block to 12½" × 12½".

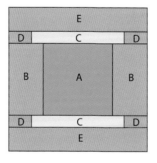

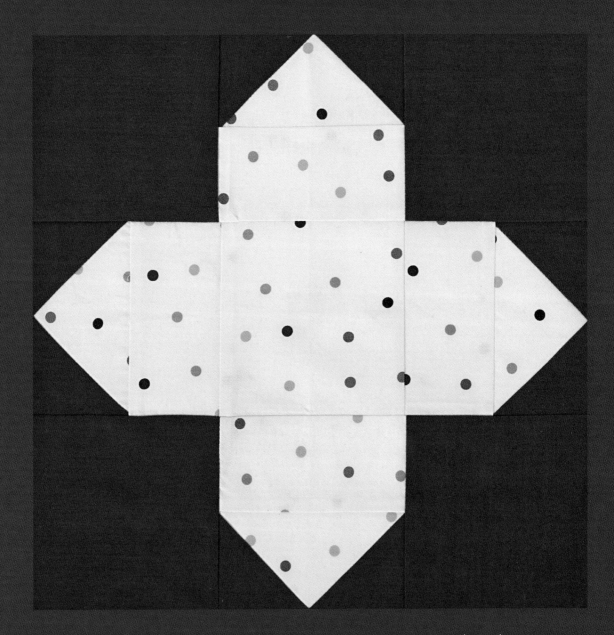

designed by Amanda Sasikirana

STACKED **SQUARES**

I got the inspiration for this block after seeing a carpet by Jonathan Adler. He is mostly known for his wonderful pottery, but he also makes great home furnishings and accessories. I was intrigued by the geometric design of one his carpets. Make this in multiples and you'll start seeing squares stacked everywhere!

SUPPLIES AND CUTTING

Green fabric

Cut 4 squares 4½″ × 4½″ for the corners.

Cut 8 squares 2½″ × 2½″.

White print fabric

Cut 1 square 4½″ × 4½″ for the center.

Cut 8 rectangles 2½″ × 4½″.

HOW-TO

Use ¼″ seam allowances.

1. Use a 2½″ × 4½″ white print rectangle and 2½″ × 2½″ green squares to make a Flying Geese unit (page 67). Make 4.

2. With right sides together, sew each Flying Geese unit to a 2½″ × 4½″ white print rectangle. Press the seam toward the white rectangle. Make 4.

3. With right sides together, sew the block pieces into 3 rows as shown. Press. Sew the rows together. Press.

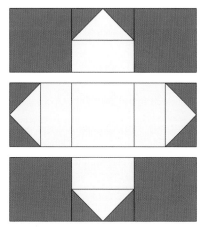

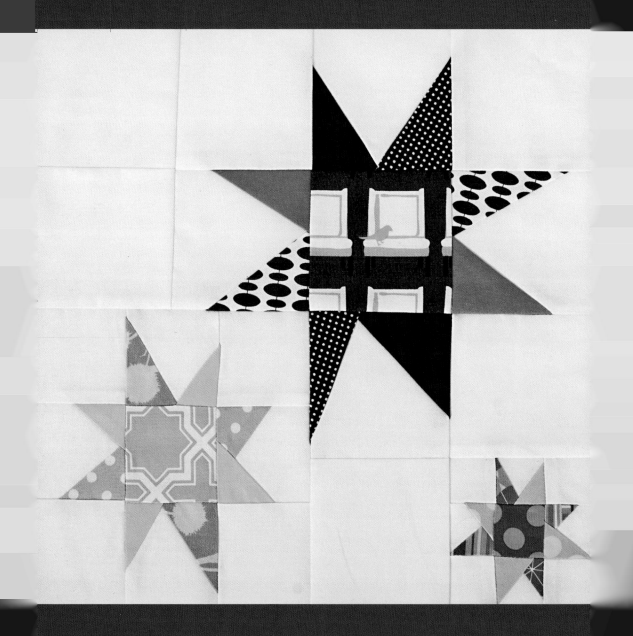

STARGAZING

designed by
Angela Pingel

This trio of differently sized wonky stars is a great addition to anyone's collection
star blocks. The uneven edges of the star points cause the stars to almost twinkle
the block. The block looks great when combined with other similarly made stars
arger sizes. Try a quilt with some stars the size of the block and some of this blo
The combination is fantastic!

SUPPLIES AND CUTTING

White fabric

Cut 10 squares 3½″ × 3½″ (A).

Cut 8 squares 1½″ × 1½″ (B).

Cut 8 squares 2½″ × 2½″ (C).

Star centers (Each square can be a different fabric.)

Cut 1 square 3½″ × 3½″ (D).

Cut 1 square 1½″ × 1½″ (E).

Cut 1 square 2½″ × 2½″ (F).

Star points (Each square can be a different fabric.)

Cut 4 squares 4″ × 4″. Cut in half on the diagonal (G).

Cut 4 squares 2″ × 2″. Cut in half on the diagonal (H).

Cut 4 squares 3″ × 3″. Cut in half on the diagonal (I).

HOW-TO

Use ¼″ seam allowances.

STAR POINTS

1. With rights sides together, place a star point triangle H on a background square B so the long edge is at a diagonal angle. Be sure that when folded back, the triangle will overlap the edges of the background square. Sew along the long edge of the triangle; then open the triangle and press.

2. Fold the triangle back and trim away the extra background fabric, leaving a ¼″ seam allowance.

3. Repeat to add another triangle to an adjacent corner. Trim the unit to 1½″ × 1½″.

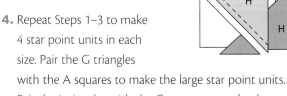

4. Repeat Steps 1–3 to make 4 star point units in each size. Pair the G triangles with the A squares to make the large star point units. Pair the I triangles with the C squares to make the medium star point units.

MAKING THE BLOCK

1. With right sides together, sew the smallest star together as you would a Nine-Patch. Press and square it to 3½″ × 3½″.

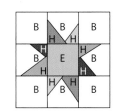

2. With right sides together, sew the blocks adjacent to the smallest star. Press and square it to 6½″ × 6½″.

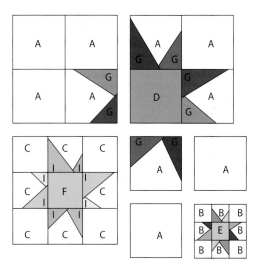

3. Make the medium-size star using the same method as for the smallest star (Step 1). Press and square it to 6½″ × 6½″.

4. With right sides together, sew the blocks together that form the upper right and left quadrants. Press and square them to 6½″ × 6½″.

5. With right sides together, sew the quadrants together.

6. Press and trim the block to 12½″ × 12½″.

designed by Heather Bostic

STONE **CATHEDRAL**

One of the most striking quilt blocks is the Cathedral Window.
With its stained-glass appearance and signature crescent curves, it combines a
classy design with a pop of color. The two complementary aspects of this quilt block
design easily carry over to a modern combination when using urban color values. In
whatever size quilt you make, this block is sure to command attention.

SUPPLIES AND CUTTING

Gray fabric

Cut 4 squares 13″ × 13″.

4 print fabrics

Cut 1 square 3½″ × 3½″ from each fabric.

HOW-TO

PREPARING THE BACKGROUND FABRIC

1. With the wrong side up, mark 1″ from each corner of a 13″ × 13″ gray square and fold each corner in on the diagonal between the marks.

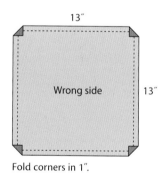

Fold corners in 1″.

2. Fold all the raw edges of the 13″ × 13″ square inward ½″ and press. *Note: All the corners should have folded miters.*

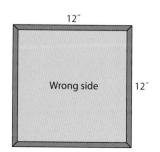

Fold sides in ½″.

3. Fold the square in half 2 times and press to create a pressed fold guide. Then unfold.

4. Fold all 4 corners inward so they meet in the center of the square. Press.

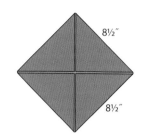

5. Repeat Step 4, bringing all 4 corners to meet in the center to create a 6″ × 6″ folded unit.

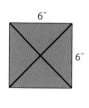

6. Repeat Steps 1–5 with the remaining 13″ × 13″ fabric squares to make 4 folded units.

SEWING THE WINDOWS

Backstitch at the beginning and end of all seams.

1. Place 2 of the 6″ × 6″ folded units back to back (flat side to flat side). Unfold 1 folded triangle from each block. Using the pressed fold as a guide, sew the units together.

Stitch.

2. Repeat Step 1 with the 2 remaining 6″ × 6″ folded units.

Sew the 2 rows of 2 previously attached folded units in the same manner. This will create a 12″ × 12″ block prepared for your window fabric.

3. Place and pin a 3½″ × 3½″ print fabric square inside each of the 4 center diamonds of the 12″ × 12″ block.

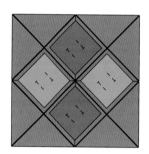

4. Starting with a center window, roll one of the 4 folded-edge borders over the backing fabric onto the window fabric so the thickest part of the roll is in the middle of the window fabric square. Secure with a pin to hold it in place. Then insert a pin into the top and bottom of the same folded edge to create a crescent shape. Refer to the block photo (page 180) as a reference.

5. Position your sewing machine's needle at the top of the background fabric curve and topstitch the edge of the curve of the first window. Backstitch at the start and end of each crescent.

6. Repeat Steps 4 and 5 throughout the block until all the curves are stitched.

STONE CATHEDRAL

181

STONEHENGE
designed by
Amy Ellis

This block makes for a fun repeat! If you are making a whole quilt from this block,
consider alternating the fabrics in the blocks by switching the placement.
Alternating would create great movement within the quilt top.
Also consider strip piecing if you are making more than one block.

SUPPLIES AND CUTTING

Blue fabric

Cut 4 rectangles 1½" × 4½" (A).

Cut 1 square 4½" × 4½" (G).

Cut 8 squares 2" × 2" (D).

White fabric

Cut 4 rectangles 1½" × 4½" (A).

Cut 4 squares 2" × 3" (B).

Cut 4 rectangles 2" × 1½" (C).

Cut 2 rectangles 2" × 7½" (E).

Cut 2 rectangles 3½" × 4½" (F).

Cut 2 rectangles 2" × 4½" (H).

HOW-TO

Use ¼" seam allowances.

1. Arrange all the cut pieces as shown.

2. Working from left to right and top to bottom, right sides together, sew the pieces into rows. Press toward the darker fabric.

3. With right sides together, sew the rows together, carefully matching the seams as needed.

4. Press and trim the block to 12½" × 12½".

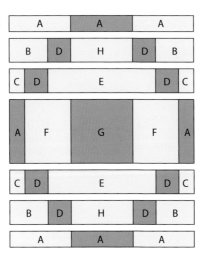

designed by Kate Henderson

STUCK IN THE **MIDDLE**

This block is a modern take on a traditional Log Cabin block.
It is made up of many different sizes of rectangles and is very simple to construct—
just add each piece in the correct order. This block would also look great
using scraps of fabric in a consistent colorway.

SUPPLIES AND CUTTING

Red fabric

Cut 1 rectangle 2½″ × 4½″ (A).

Blue fabric

Cut 1 rectangle 5½″ × 3½″ (B).

Cut 2 rectangles 2″ × 3½″ (C).

Brown fabric

Cut 2 rectangles 2″ × 3½″ (D).

Cut 1 rectangle 3″ × 8″ (E).

Cut 1 rectangle 1½″ × 8″ (F).

Cut 1 square 2½″ × 2½″ (G).

Green fabric

Cut 1 rectangle 5½″ × 2″ (H).

Cut 1 rectangle 1½″ × 3½″ (I).

Cut 1 rectangle 3″ × 3½″ (J).

Cut 1 rectangle 9″ × 2″ (K).

Cut 1 rectangle 2½″ × 12½″ (L).

Cut 1 rectangle 2″ × 12½″ (M).

HOW-TO

Use ¼″ seam allowances.

1. With right sides together, sew the center section together as shown. Press as you go.

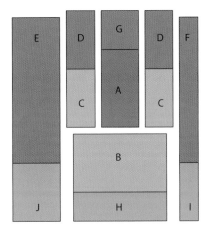

2. With right sides together, sew the top (K) and side (L and M) borders to the center section. Press.

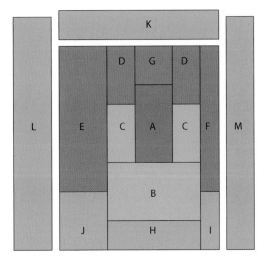

3. Trim the block to 12½″ × 12½″.

THREE **WISHES** designed by Jamie Moilanen

This is a fun, wonky star block that contains three stars in one.
It starts with a small star that makes up the center of the second star,
which makes up the center of the largest star. This is a great block
to use up scraps along with a single background color.

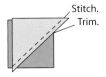
SUPPLIES AND CUTTING

Pink fabric for background

Cut 8 squares 1½" × 1½" for the small star.

Cut 8 squares 3½" × 3½" for the medium star.

Cut 4 squares 2" × 2" for the corners.

Cut 4 strips 2" × 9½" for the large star.

Assorted print fabrics for star points

For the small star:

Cut 1 square 1½" × 1½".

Cut 4 squares 1½" × 1½". Cut each square in half on the diagonal.

For the medium star:

Cut 4 squares 3½" × 3½". Cut each square in half on the diagonal.

For the large star:

Cut 4 rectangles 2½" × 7" (can be all one or a mix of prints). Cut each rectangle in half on the diagonal.

HOW-TO

Use ¼" seam allowances.

FOR THE SMALL STAR

1. With right sides together, place a 1½" triangle at an angle on a 1½" × 1½" pink background square as shown. Stitch along the long side of the triangle and trim the excess background square.

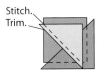
Stitch.
Trim.

2. Press the first triangle open. With right sides together, place another print triangle on the background square at an angle. Stitch along the long side of the triangle and trim the seam allowance.

Stitch.
Trim.

3. Press the second triangle open and trim the star point unit to 1½" × 1½".

4. Repeat Steps 1–3 to make 4 small star point units.

5. Arrange the 4 star point units and 4 remaining 1½" × 1½" pink squares as shown. Place the 1½" × 1½" print square in the middle. With right sides together, stitch the squares and units into rows; then stitch the rows together. Trim the nine-patch unit to 3½" × 3½".

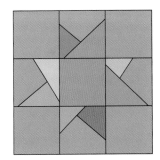

FOR THE MEDIUM STAR

Repeat Steps 1–4 above with the 3½" print triangles and 3½" square solid background squares to create 4 medium star point units. Trim each unit to 3½" × 3½". Arrange the medium star point units and the 4 remaining 3½" background squares into a nine-patch layout. Use the small nine-patch unit from Step 5 as the center square. Sew as a nine-patch unit. Press and trim to 9½" × 9½".

FOR THE LARGE STAR

Create 4 large star point units using the process in Steps 1–3 with the triangles from the 2½" × 7" print rectangles and the 2" × 9½" background rectangles. Trim each large star point unit to 2½" × 9½". Form a nine-patch layout with the medium star in the middle, the large star point units on the 4 sides and the 2" squares in the corners (see block photo, page 196). Sew as a nine-patch. Press and trim to 12½" × 12½".

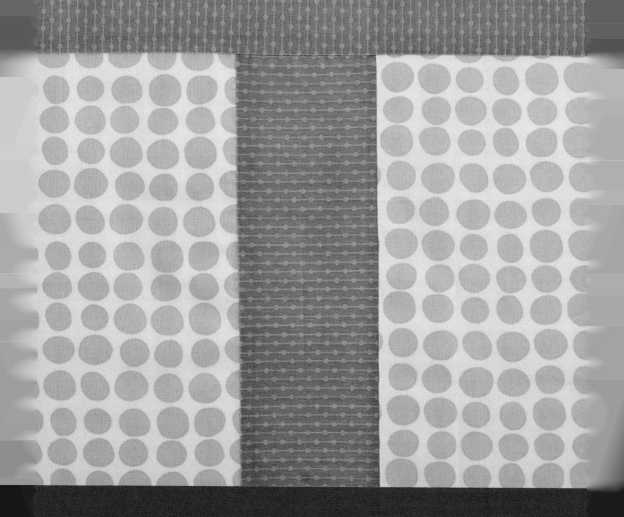

TO A T

designed by
Cheryl Arkison

Modern quilting is inherently bold, graphic, and simple.
is block is definitely modern. Made from just four pieces of fabric, it combines in
quilt to a stunning effect. Rotate the blocks as you set them for the strongest impa

SUPPLIES AND CUTTING

Orange fabric

Cut 1 strip 3½" × 9½".

Cut 1 strip 12½" × 3½".

Turquoise fabric

Cut 2 rectangles 5" × 9½".

HOW-TO

Use ¼" seam allowances.

1. With right sides together, sew the 3½" × 9½" strip of orange fabric between the 5" × 9½" turquoise pieces. Press toward the orange strip. The assembled unit should measure 12½" × 9½".

2. Sew the 12½" × 3½" orange strip to the top of the pieced unit from Step 1. Press toward the long orange strip. Trim the block to 12½" × 12½".

TOPSY-TURVY **TREE**

designed by
Nicole Kaplan

This whimsical block features a tree foundation pieced in a wonky Log Cabin style.
Square up the units by trimming off excess fabric as you go. You can also angle the
ruler during the trimming process to create fun, off-kilter effects. This landscape block
is perfect for using up scraps and experimenting with new designs!

SUPPLIES AND CUTTING

Green fabrics for treetop unit

Cut 1 trapezoid approximately 3″ × 3½″ (treetop 1).

Cut 8–10 strips 2½″ × 8″ (treetops 4, 5, 6, 7, 10c, and 11).

Cut 3 strips 1½″ × 3″ (treetops 2, 3, and 10a).

Yellow print for birds

Cut 1 square 2½″ × 2½″ (treetop 10b).

White fabric for sky

Cut 2 rectangles 3″ × 7″ (treetops 9 and 12).

Cut 1 rectangle 3″ × 13″ (treetop 13).

Cut 1 rectangle 6″ × 5″ (lower left 1).

Cut 1 rectangle 6″ × 2″ (lower right 3).

Cut 1 square 3″ × 3″. Cut in half on the diagonal to make 2 triangles (treetop 8 and lower right 5).

Brown fabric for trunk

Cut 1 rectangle 2½″ × 7″ (lower left 3).

Cut 1 rectangle 1¼″ × 5″ (lower right 4).

Novelty print for gnome

Cut 1 rectangle 3½″ × 8″ (lower right 2).

Blue fabrics for ground

Cut 1 rectangle 6″ × 4″ (lower left 2).

Cut 1 rectangle 8″ × 4″ (lower right 1).

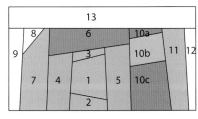

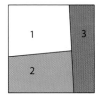 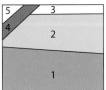

HOW-TO

The foundation pattern is on page 220.

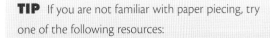

> **TIP** If you are not familiar with paper piecing, try one of the following resources:
>
> · *Every Quilter's Foundation Piecing Reference Tool* by Jane Hall and Dixie Haywood
>
> · *Carol Doak Teaches You to Paper Piece* DVD

TREETOP UNIT

1. Foundation piece the treetop unit. Trim and press as you go. Note that 10a, 10b, and 10c need to be sewn together before they are sewn to the pieced unit.

2. Trim the treetop unit to 12½″ × 7″. Set aside.

LOWER LEFT UNIT

1. Foundation piece the lower left section, adding the pieces in numerical order. Trim and press as you go.

2. Trim to 6″ × 6″. Set aside.

LOWER RIGHT UNIT

1. Foundation piece the lower right section, adding the pieces in numerical order. Trim and press as you go.

2. Trim the pieced unit to 7″ × 6″. Set aside.

BLOCK ASSEMBLY

1. With right sides together, sew the lower left section to the lower right section. Press and trim to 12½″ × 6″.

2. With right sides together, sew the treetop section to the lower section created in Step 1. Press and trim to 12½″ × 12½″. Carefully remove the foundation paper.

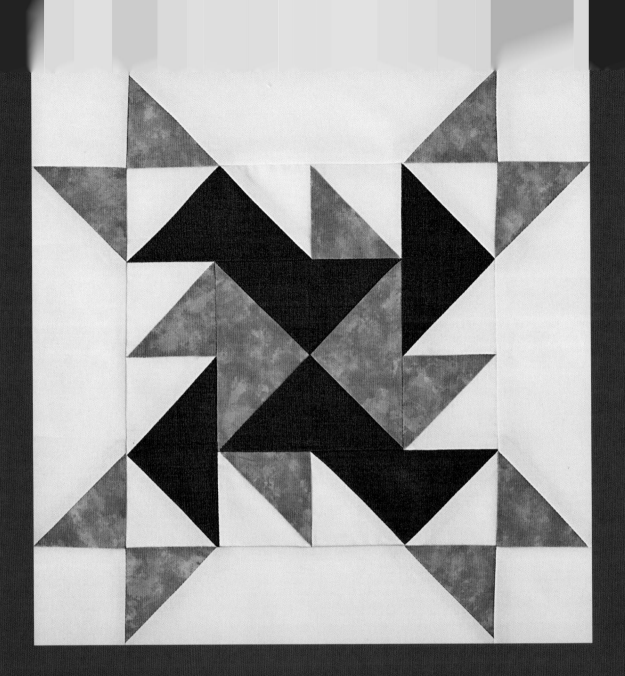

TURNAROUND

designed by
Monique Dillard

This block is a traditional block using Flying Geese, half-square triangles, and a quarter-square triangle. Flying Geese are one of my favorite piecing techniques. I love the way they create the two half-square triangles with no seam.

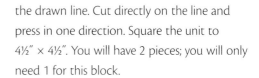

SUPPLIES AND CUTTING

White fabric

Cut 2 squares 2⅞" × 2⅞".

Cut 12 squares 2½" × 2½".

Cut 4 rectangles 2½" × 8½".

Green fabric

Cut 2 squares 2⅞" × 2⅞".

Cut 1 square 5¼" × 5¼".

Cut 8 squares 2½" × 2½".

Red fabric

Cut 1 square 5¼" × 5¼".

Cut 4 rectangles 2½" × 4½".

HOW-TO

Use ¼" seam allowances.

1. Make 4 half-square triangle units (page 27) from 2 white 2⅞" × 2⅞" squares and 2 green 2⅞" × 2⅞" squares.

2. Make 4 Flying Geese (page 67) using 8 white 2½" × 2½" squares and the 4 red 2½" × 4½" rectangles.

3. With right sides together, sew the Flying Geese from Step 2 to the half-square triangle units from Step 1. Press toward the half-square triangle units.

4. Make half-square triangle units from the green 5¼" × 5¼" square and the red 5¼" × 5¼" square. On the back of one of the half-square triangle units, draw a diagonal line from corner to corner, bisecting the seam. Place the drawn square right sides together on the other half-square triangle, rotating the top piece so that opposite colors meet. Sew ¼" on either side of the drawn line. Cut directly on the line and press in one direction. Square the unit to 4½" × 4½". You will have 2 pieces; you will only need 1 for this block.

5. With right sides together, sew the center of the block together as shown. Note that the first piece is sewn only halfway. After adding piece 4, complete the first seam. Square the piece to 8½" × 8½".

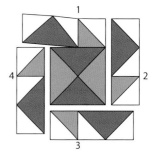

6. On the back of each of the 8 green 2½" × 2½" squares, draw a diagonal line from corner to corner. With right sides together, place a green square 2½" × 2½" on the end of a white 2½" × 8½" rectangle. Sew on the drawn line and trim the seam allowance to ¼". Sew another green 2½" × 2½" square on the other end as shown. Make sure the drawn lines are angled in the correct direction. Make 4.

7. With right sides together, sew the block together as shown. Square the block to 12½" × 12½".

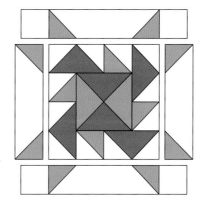

TWO BY **SIX** designed by Natalie Hardin

This is a great way for the improvisational or modern quilter to use favorite scraps left over from other projects. You're not required to cut each piece to a particular shape, so you get a unique block every time. Don't worry if you think you made a mistake. In fact, because it's random construction, a little error may work in your favor! Experiment with the number of scraps, angles, and even your color scheme. Once you make one, you won't want to stop.

SUPPLIES AND CUTTING

Assorted red fabrics

Cut 6–8 pieces about 10″ × 4″ for horizontal strips.

Cut 2–3 pieces about 3″ × 13″ for vertical strips.

Note: To add originality, consider using scraps that are already sewn together to meet the measurements above.

HOW-TO

Use ¼″ seam allowances.

1. With right sides together, sew the 10″ × 4″ horizontal pieces together at any angles you choose. Press the seams open. Trim the pieced unit to 8½″ × 12½″.

2. Sew the 3″ × 13″ vertical pieces together as you did the horizontal pieces in Step 1. Press the seams open. Trim the pieced unit to 4½″ × 12½″.

3. With right sides together, sew the pieced units together as shown in the block photo (page 194). Press the seam open.

4. Trim the block to 12½″ × 12½″.

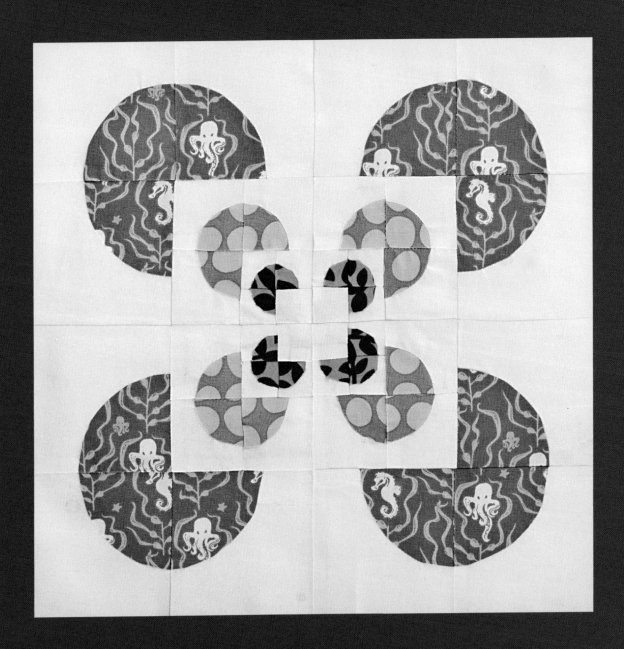

WEDGED **IN**

designed by
Briana Arlene Balsam

If you look closely, you'll see that this block is a spin-off of the traditional
Drunkard's Path block. It is composed of three sizes of quarter-circle pieces
that appear to be popping out of one another. Play with different hues
of the same color of fabric to create a three-dimensional effect or use
different fabric prints for each quarter-circle unit to create a scrappy look.

SUPPLIES AND CUTTING

Template patterns are on pages 218 and 219.

Dark blue fabric

Cut 12 squares 1″ × 1″.

Light blue fabric

Cut 12 squares 1½″ × 1½″. Trace and cut out 12 using Template B and the 1½″ × 1½″ light blue squares.

Orange fabric

Cut 12 squares 2½″ × 2½″. Trace and cut out 12 using Template C and the 2½″ × 2½″ orange squares.

White fabric

Cut 16 squares 1¼″ × 1¼″.

Cut 12 squares 2″ × 2″. Trace and cut out 12 using Template D and the 2″ × 2″ white squares.

Cut 12 squares 3½″ × 3½″. Trace and cut out 12 using Template E and the 3½″ × 3½″ white squares.

Freezer paper

HOW-TO

Use ¼″ seam allowances.

1. Trace 12 of Template A onto freezer paper and cut out. Iron the pieces onto the 1″ × 1″ dark blue squares and cut out, adding a ¼″ seam allowance *only* on the curved edge.

2. Fold over and iron or hand baste the curved edges of the dark blue pieces over the freezer paper.

3. Place the dark blue pieces on the 1¼″ × 1¼″ white squares, lining up the 90° angle of each dark blue piece with one corner of a white square. Appliqué *only* the curved side of the dark blue piece.

4. With right sides together, pin and sew each light blue B to a white D, easing the fabric as necessary to avoid puckering around the curved edge. Press toward the light blue.

5. With right sides together, pin and sew each orange C to a white E, easing the fabric as necessary to avoid puckering around the curved edge. Press toward the orange.

6. Assemble the block pieces in quadrants, working from the center outward as shown, pressing as you go. Make 4 quadrants.

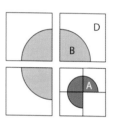

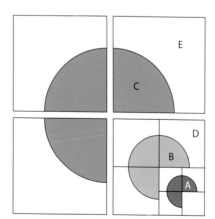

Upper left quadrant

7. Sew the assembled quadrants together. Press and trim to 12½″ × 12½″.

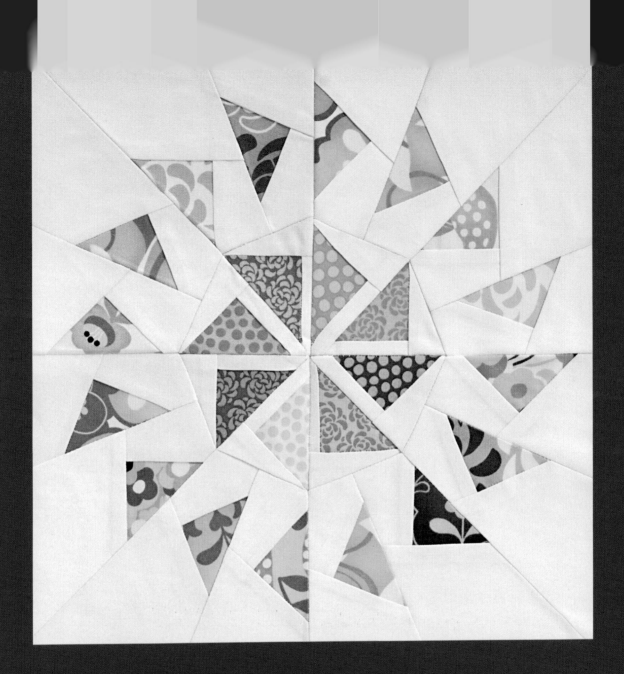

WINDMILL

designed by
Lynne Goldsworthy

This block is striking if made with various patterned fabrics
against a solid background. It also works well with a spectrum of fabrics
against a solid. Paper piecing the segments is very simple and gives lovely
sharp points. Piecing together the 24 segments requires some care
to match the seams and corners for maximum impact.

SUPPLIES AND CUTTING

White fabric for background

This block requires 1–1½ fat quarters of the solid background, depending on how efficient your paper piecing is. I cut the fabric as required as I go, though you may find it quicker and easier to first cut the fabric into widths of 2″ and 3″ to be used as required.

Scraps of colored fabric for triangles

Cut 24 rectangles 2″ × 3½″ for foundation piecing. Scraps left over from trimming half-square triangles can also be perfect for this.

Foundation paper, such as Simple Foundations Translucent Vellum Paper or Carol Doak's Foundation Paper

HOW-TO

The paper-piecing pattern is on page 221.

> **TIP** If you are not familiar with paper piecing, try one of the following resources:
>
> · *Every Quilter's Foundation Piecing Reference Tool* by Jane Hall and Dixie Haywood
>
> · *Carol Doak Teaches You to Paper Piece* DVD

1. Copy or trace the pattern 4 times to make the 4 quadrant templates required for the block.

2. Place the 4 templates on a table and place your scraps of colored fabric on the 4 templates in a pleasing order. Write on the template where each fabric will go (remembering that the circles of Flying Geese will fly clockwise once the block is finished, as you piece the block on the reverse).

3. Separate each of the 4 quadrant templates into 6 segments as shown. Paper piece each of the 24 segments, remembering to use small stitches (set your machine stitch length to around 1.5) and to leave a seam allowance of at least ¼″ around each pattern section.

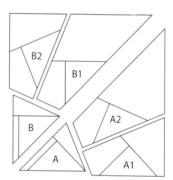

4. Trim the seam allowances around each section to ¼″, change your stitch length back to whatever you normally use for piecing, and assemble each quadrant as shown.

5. Sew the 4 quadrants together, using the block photo (page 198) as a reference. Carefully tear off all the paper from the back of the finished block; it should tear quite easily along the perforations made by the small stitches. Trim the block to 12½″ × 12½″.

WINNER'S **CIRCLE** designed by Elizabeth Scott

Here's a winning way to frame a favorite photo.

SUPPLIES AND CUTTING

Trace the shapes from the block photo (page 200) and enlarge by 200%.

Black print fabric

Cut 1 square 13" × 13". Trim to 12½" × 12½" after appliqué.

Photo on fabric

Print your chosen photo onto fabric. Cut around the photo in a circle 5¼" in diameter.

Yellow print fabric

Cut 1 scalloped outer circle.

Green print fabric

Cut 2 ribbon tails.

Black solid fabric

Cut 1 scalloped inner circle.

Paper-backed fusible web

HOW-TO

1. Trace the enlarged shapes onto the paper side of the fusible web. Cut out the shapes from the fusible web, approximately ¼" outside the drawn lines.

2. Iron the fusible web shapes (following the manufacturer's instructions) onto the wrong side of the appliqué fabric. Cut out the fabric pieces on the drawn lines and peel off the backing paper.

3. Arrange and fuse the fabric pieces onto the black background square in the following order: yellow scalloped outer circle, photo, and black scalloped inner circle. Slide the 2 green ribbon tails under the edge of the outer scallop. When you are pleased with the arrangement, fuse the pieces in place.

4. Stitch around the raw edges of the pieces by hand or machine. Trim the block to 12½" × 12½".

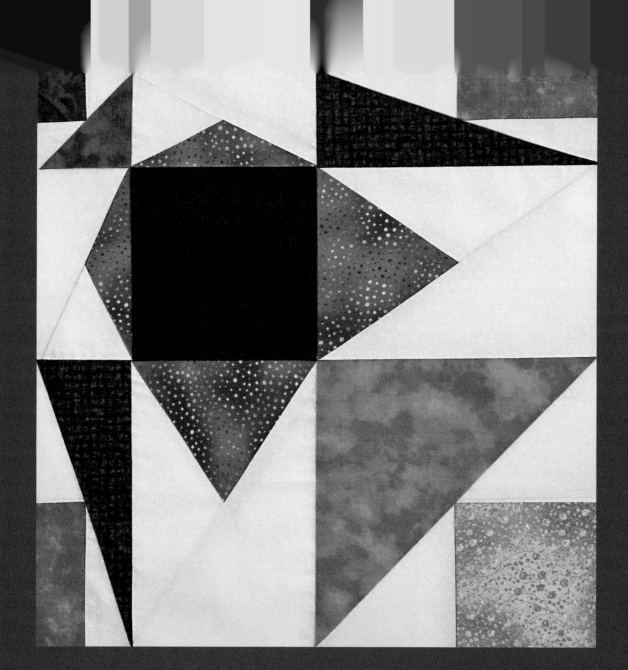

designed by Wayne Kollinger

WONKY AUNT DINAH

Repeat, rotate, or reflect this block to create exciting designs.

SUPPLIES AND CUTTING

Enlarge the pattern on page 222 by 200%. Use a Sharpie Ultra Fine Point pen to trace the pattern onto the shiny side of the freezer paper. Carefully cut the freezer paper pattern apart to create the templates. Press the shiny side of the freezer paper onto the wrong side of each fabric. Cut out each piece, adding an exact ¼″ seam allowance to all sides.

5″ × 5″ dark purple fabric

Cut B4.

6″ × 7″ medium purple fabric

Cut A11 and C4.

4″ × 4″ light purple fabric

Cut A8 and C1.

2″ × 2″ dark pink fabric

Cut A1.

3″ × 3″ medium pink fabric

Cut A4.

5″ × 12″ pink fabric

Cut A5 and B1.

Cut B5 and C5.

7″ × 7″ light pink fabric

Cut C11.

4″ × 4″ pale pink fabric

Cut C8.

¼ yard or 1 fat quarter (18″ × 22″) white fabric

Cut A2, A3, A6, A7, A9, A10, B2, B3, B6, B7, C2, C3, C6, C7, C9, and C10.

HOW-TO

Use ¼″ seam allowances.

1. Arrange all the pieces as shown. Check that they are all there and cut correctly.

2. Either leave the freezer paper on the back of the fabric and use the edge of the freezer paper as your sewing line, or draw the ¼″ seam-line on the wrong side of each piece.

3. With right sides together, pair up the pieces and poke pins through the points to ensure that they line up. Sew the pieces together to make units as shown. Press the seams open to reduce bulk.

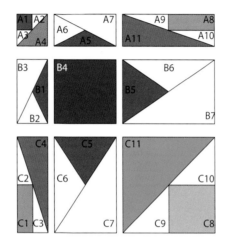

4. Sew the units into rows. Press.

5. Sew the rows together. Press. Remove freezer paper, if you have not already done so.

designed by Natasha Bruecher

YOU'VE BEEN **FRAMED**

This block is the perfect way to show off your favorite big prints and make them a feature in a quilt, pillow, or other project.

SUPPLIES AND CUTTING

Fussy-cut fabric motif

Cut 1 square 4½″ × 4½″ for
the center.

Brown fabric

Cut 2 strips 1″ × 4½″.

Cut 2 strips 5½″ × 1″.

Cut 4 strips 1″ × 2″.

Cut 4 squares 2½″ × 2½″.

White fabric

Cut 4 squares 2″ × 2″.

Cut 6 squares 2⅜″ × 2⅜″.

Orange fabric

Cut 6 squares 2⅜″ × 2⅜″.

Plum fabric

Cut 4 strips 2½″ × 8½″.

HOW-TO

Use ¼″ seam allowances.

1. With right sides together, sew 1″ × 4½″ brown
strips to the top and bottom of the center
fussy-cut square. Sew a 5½″ × 1″ brown strip to
either side of the center unit.

2. Use the 6 orange and 6 white 2⅜″ × 2⅜″ squares
to make 12 half-square triangles (page 27). Sew
3 half-square triangles in a row. Add a 1″ × 2″
brown strip to the right side of the row as
shown. Make 4 rows.

3. Sew a row from Step 2 to either side of the
center unit from Step 1. Add a 2″ × 2″ white
square to either end of the remaining 2 rows
from Step 2; then sew to the top and bottom
of the center unit.

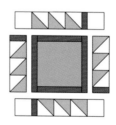

4. Add the 4 plum strips 2½″ × 8½″
and brown corner squares 2½″ × 2½″ as
shown. Trim the block to 12½″ × 12½″.

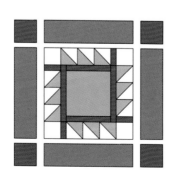

Freewheeling
– – continued from page 73 – –

9. Trim the block ¼" beyond the freezer paper on all sides so it measures 5½" × 5½".

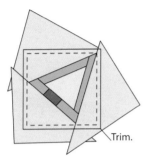

Trim ¼" beyond freezer paper.

10. Repeat Steps 3–9 for the remaining green triangle and for the 2 plum triangles, so you have 4 blocks.

11. Arrange the blocks in a 4-block pinwheel shape and sew together.

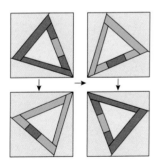

12. Cut the 1½" × 15" strips of green and plum fabric into pieces of random length. Sew these pieces together, mixing up the green and the plum. Trim to make 2 strips 1½" × 10½" and 2 strips 1½" × 12½".

13. Sew the 2 strips 1½" × 10½" to the top and bottom of the pinwheel block. Sew the 2 strips 1½" × 12½" to the sides of the block.

14. Remove the paper from the block by gently folding it back, creasing with your finger, and tearing away.

Mondrian
– – continued from page 117 – –

3. With right sides together, continue sewing the block as shown.

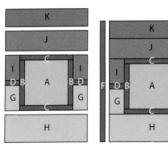

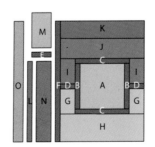

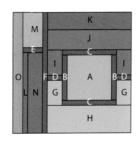

Set Sail
– – continued from page 167 – –

5. Sew the 12½" × 2½" mermaid strip to the bottom of the boat unit from Step 1. Sew this unit to the sail unit from Step 4.

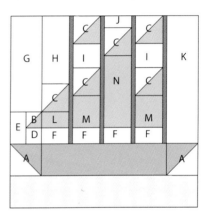

6. Reverse the flag template pattern (page 218) and trace onto the paper side of fusible web. Cut out the flag ¼" outside the pattern lines. Fuse the web onto the wrong side of the striped fabric scrap. Cut the fabric piece on the line and fuse onto the block, following the manufacturer's instructions and using the block photo (page 166) as a placement guide. Topstitch to hold the flag in place.

TEMPLATE PATTERNS

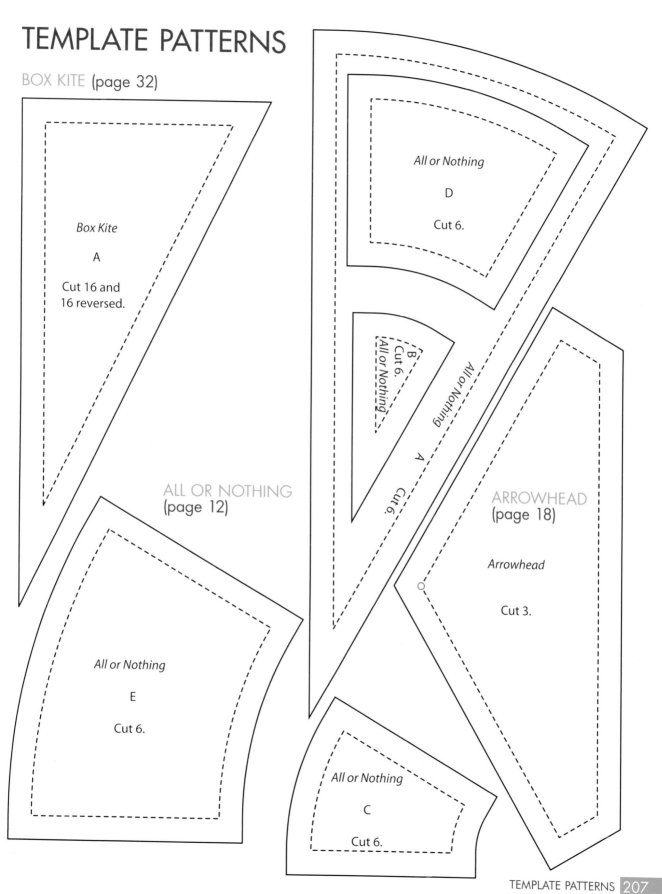

BOX KITE (page 32)

Box Kite

A

Cut 16 and
16 reversed.

All or Nothing

D

Cut 6.

All or Nothing

B
Cut 6.

All or Nothing

A
Cut 6.

ALL OR NOTHING
(page 12)

ARROWHEAD
(page 18)

Arrowhead

Cut 3.

All or Nothing

E

Cut 6.

All or Nothing

C

Cut 6.

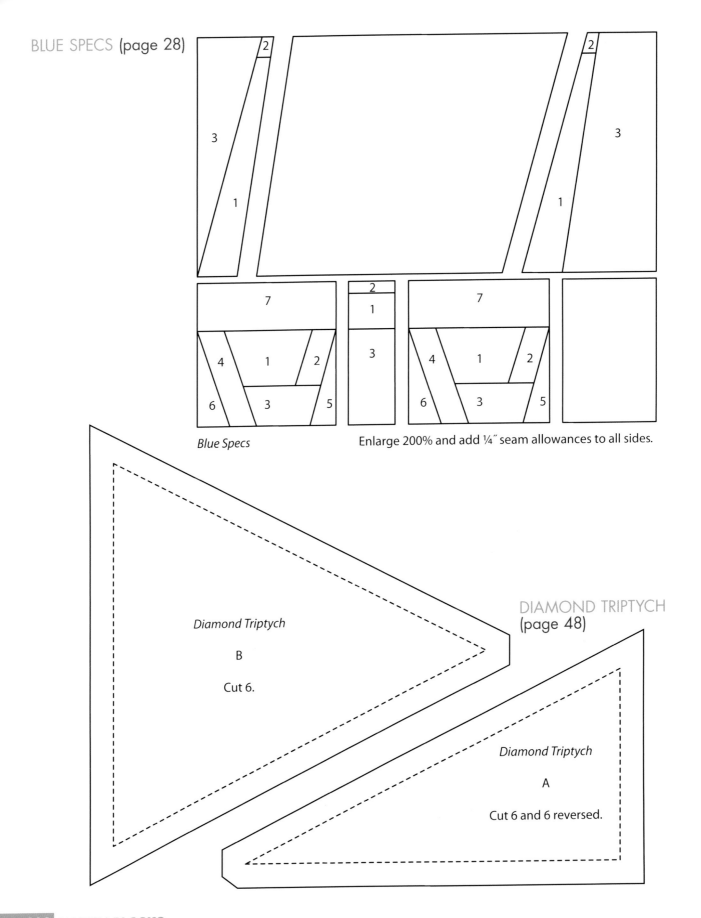

Blue Specs

Enlarge 200% and add ¼˝ seam allowances to all sides.

Diamond Triptych

B

Cut 6.

Diamond Triptych

A

Cut 6 and 6 reversed.

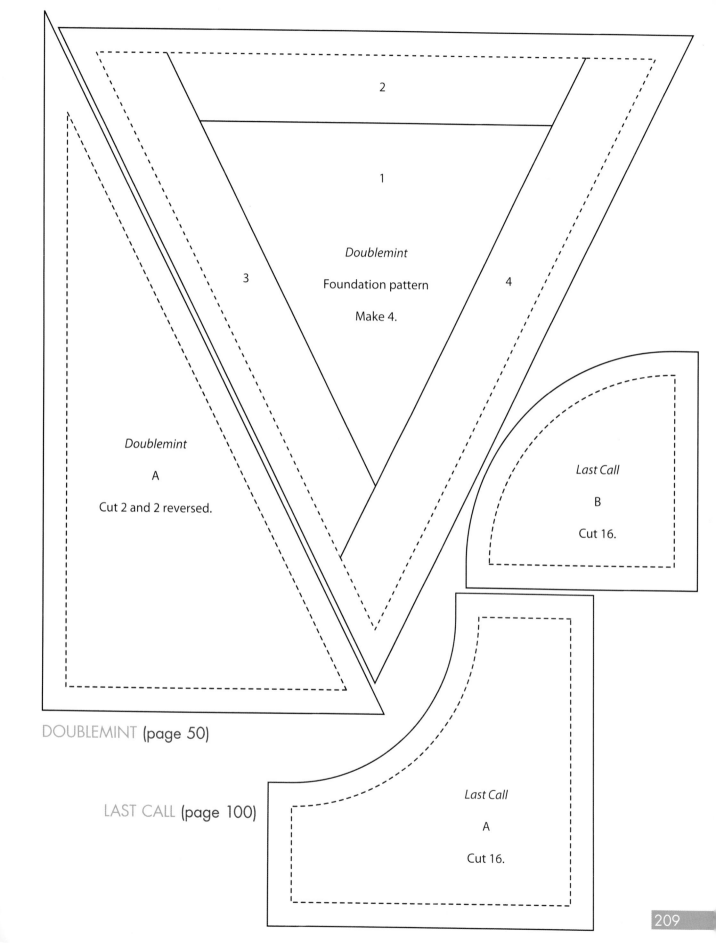

2

1

Doublemint

Foundation pattern

Make 4.

3

4

Doublemint

A

Cut 2 and 2 reversed.

Last Call

B

Cut 16.

DOUBLEMINT (page 50)

LAST CALL (page 100)

Last Call

A

Cut 16.

ECCENTRIC WONKY STAR (page 54)

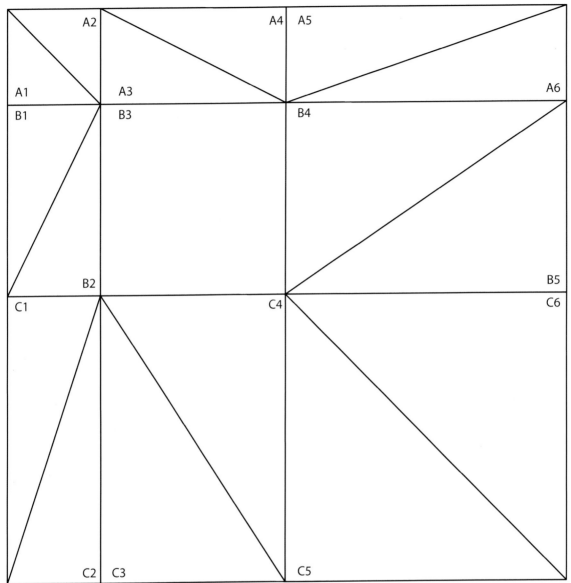

Enlarge 200% and add ¼˝ seam allowances to each piece.

Eccentric Wonky Star

EXUBERANT (page 62)

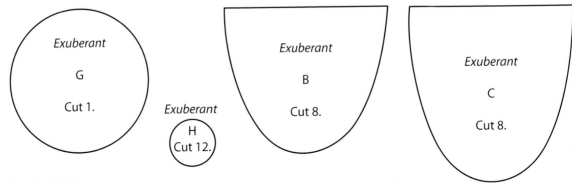

Exuberant

G

Cut 1.

Exuberant

H
Cut 12.

Exuberant

B

Cut 8.

Exuberant

C

Cut 8.

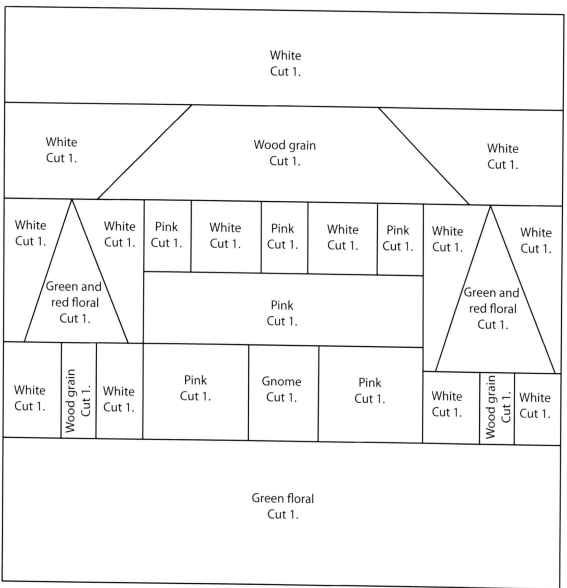

White
Cut 1.

White
Cut 1.

Wood grain
Cut 1.

White
Cut 1.

White
Cut 1.

White
Cut 1.

Pink
Cut 1.

White
Cut 1.

Pink
Cut 1.

White
Cut 1.

Pink
Cut 1.

White
Cut 1.

White
Cut 1.

Green and
red floral
Cut 1.

Pink
Cut 1.

Green and
red floral
Cut 1.

White
Cut 1.

Wood grain
Cut 1.

White
Cut 1.

Pink
Cut 1.

Gnome
Cut 1.

Pink
Cut 1.

White
Cut 1.

Wood grain
Cut 1.

White
Cut 1.

Green floral
Cut 1.

Enlarge 200% and add ¼″ seam allowances to all sides.

Gnome Home

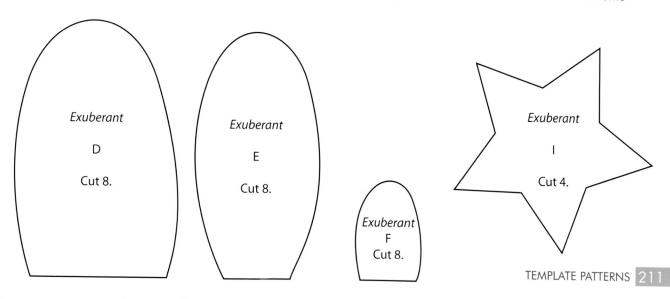

Exuberant

D

Cut 8.

Exuberant

E

Cut 8.

Exuberant
F
Cut 8.

Exuberant

I

Cut 4.

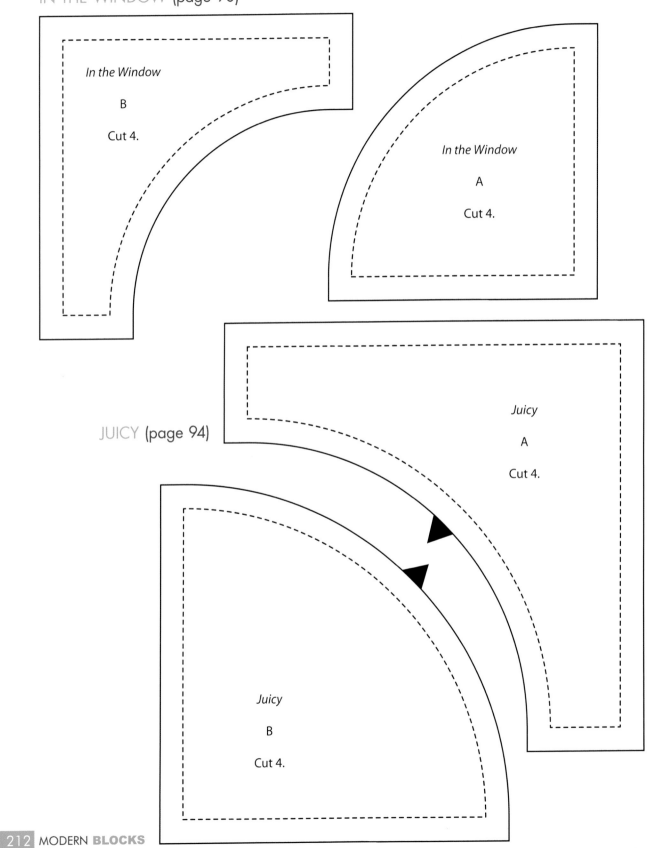

In the Window

B

Cut 4.

In the Window

A

Cut 4.

JUICY (page 94)

Juicy

A

Cut 4.

Juicy

B

Cut 4.

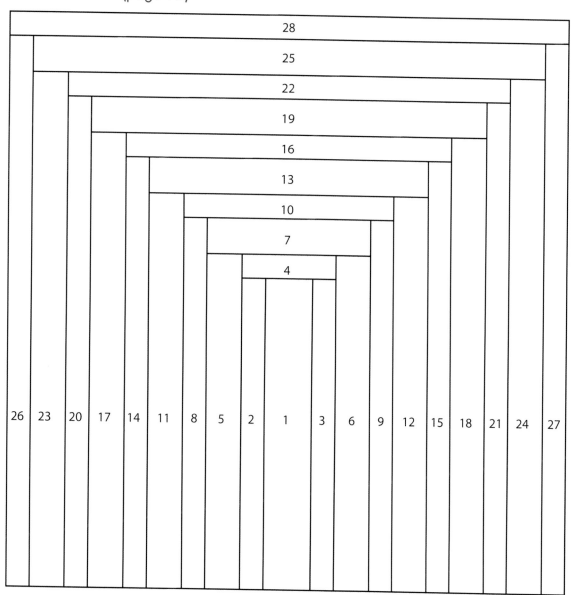

Enlarge 200% and add ¼˝ seam allowances to all sides.

It's a Stretch

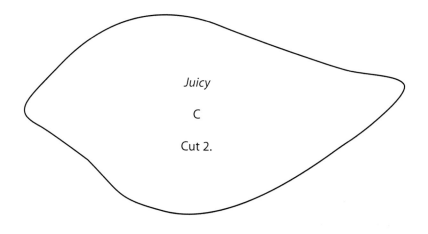

Juicy

C

Cut 2.

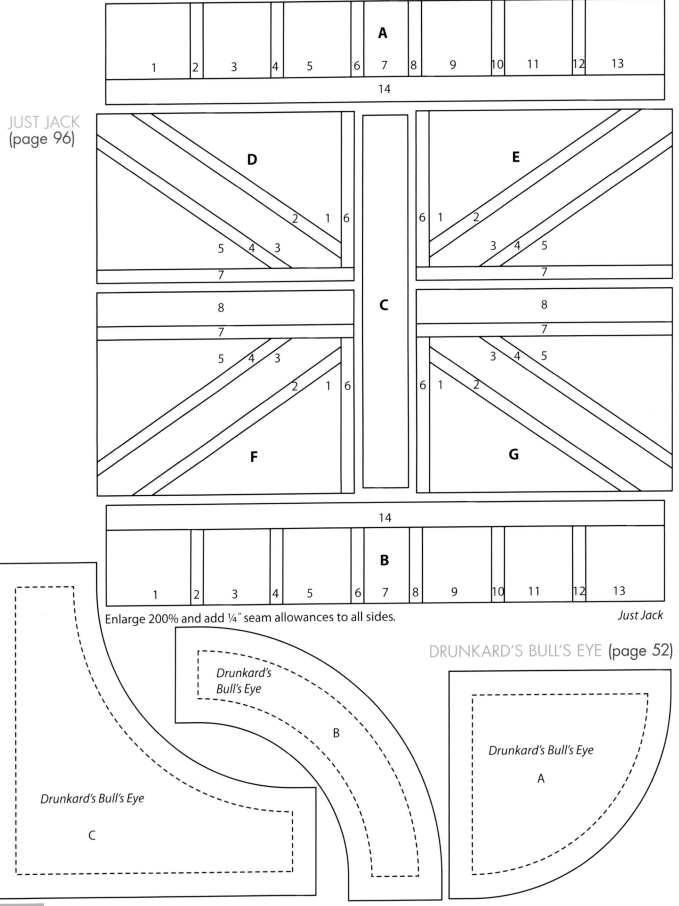

JUST JACK
(page 96)

Enlarge 200% and add ¼˝ seam allowances to all sides.

Just Jack

DRUNKARD'S BULL'S EYE (page 52)

Drunkard's Bull's Eye

B

Drunkard's Bull's Eye

A

Drunkard's Bull's Eye

C

OPEN BOOK
(page 126)

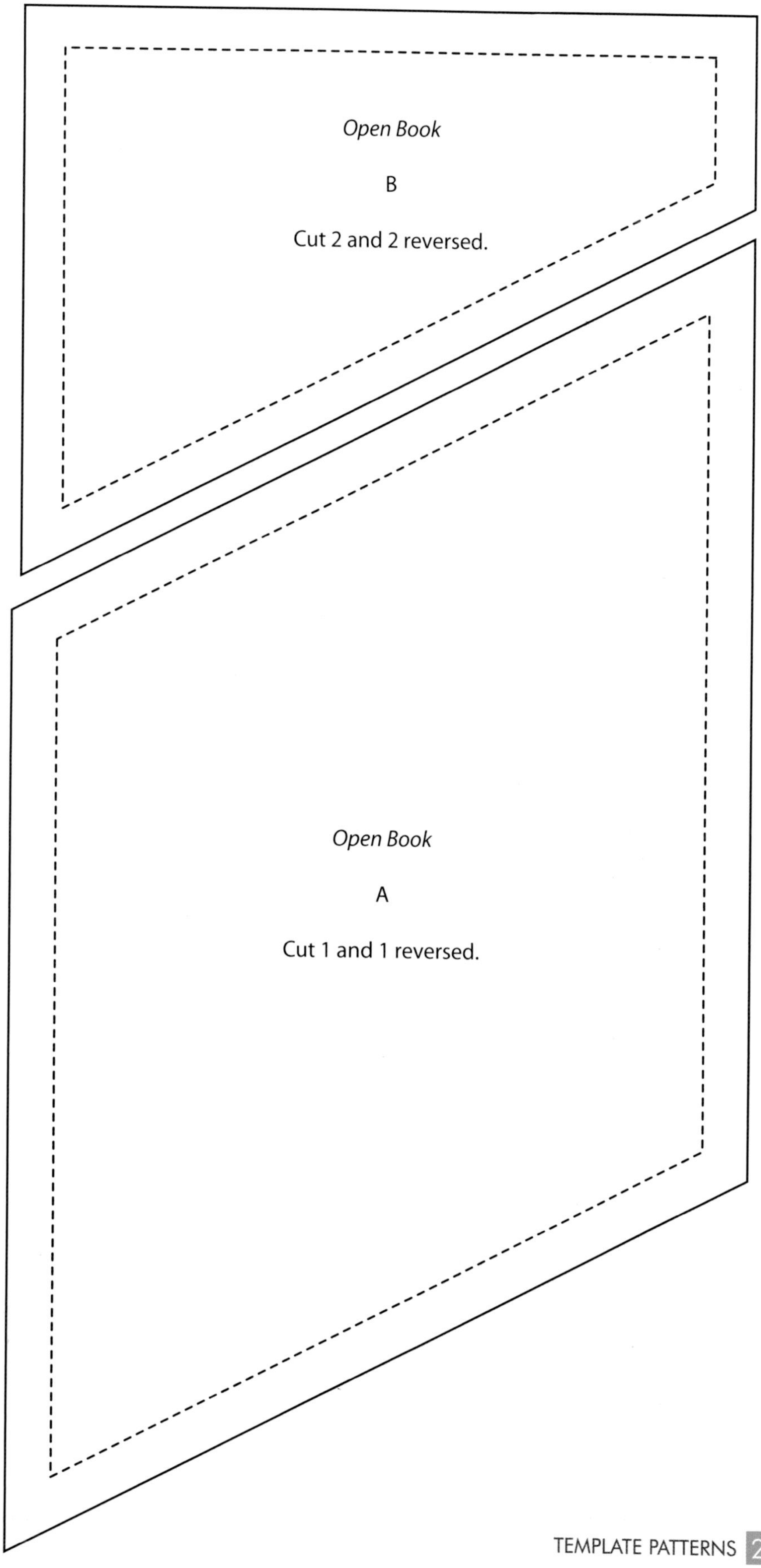

Open Book

B

Cut 2 and 2 reversed.

Open Book

A

Cut 1 and 1 reversed.

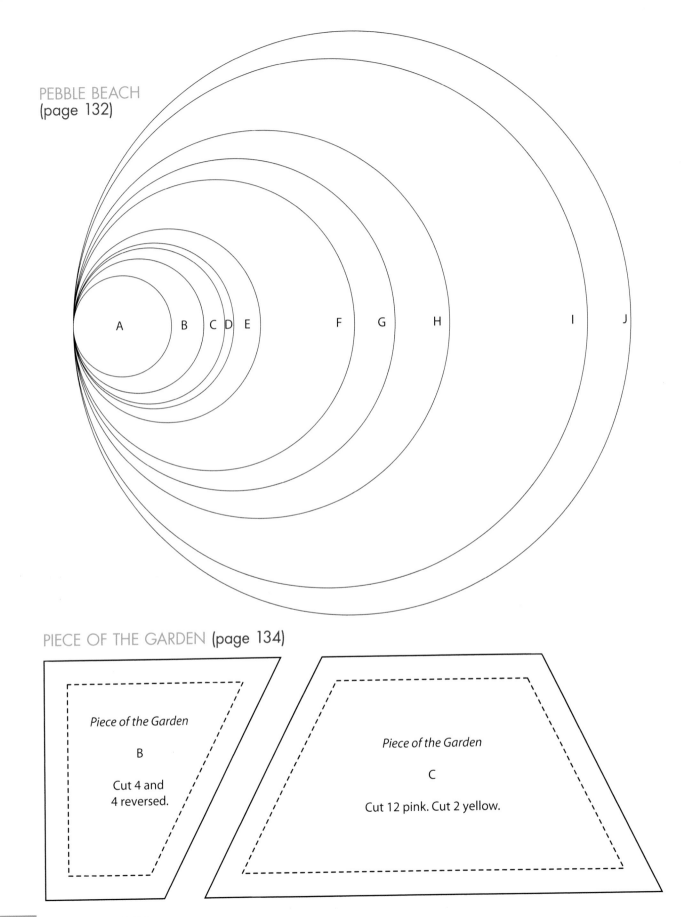

PEBBLE BEACH
(page 132)

A   B   C D E   F   G   H   I   J

PIECE OF THE GARDEN (page 134)

Piece of the Garden

B

Cut 4 and
4 reversed.

Piece of the Garden

C

Cut 12 pink. Cut 2 yellow.

QUARTER-CUT DAISY (page 148)

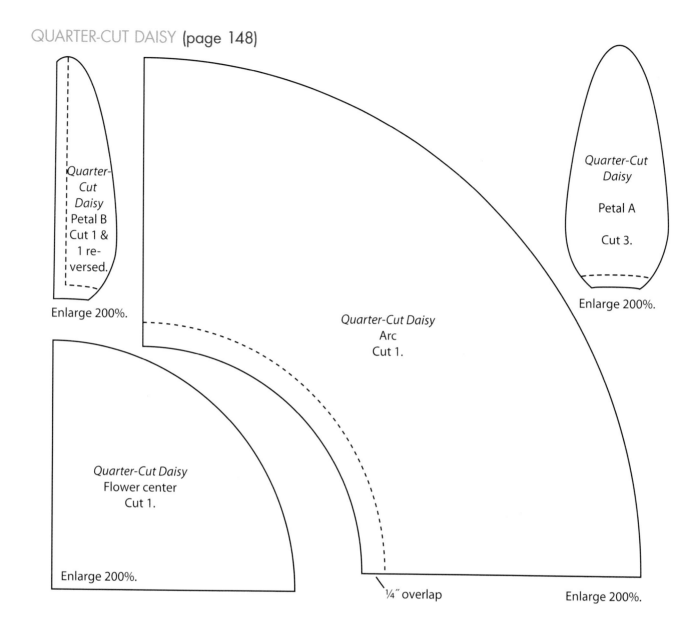

Quarter-Cut Daisy Petal B Cut 1 & 1 reversed.

Enlarge 200%.

Quarter-Cut Daisy Flower center Cut 1.

Enlarge 200%.

Quarter-Cut Daisy Arc Cut 1.

¼″ overlap

Quarter-Cut Daisy Petal A Cut 3.

Enlarge 200%.

Enlarge 200%.

PIECE OF THE GARDEN (page 134)

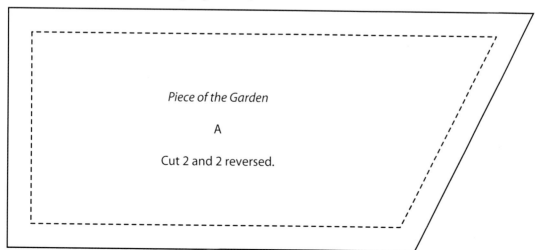

Piece of the Garden

A

Cut 2 and 2 reversed.

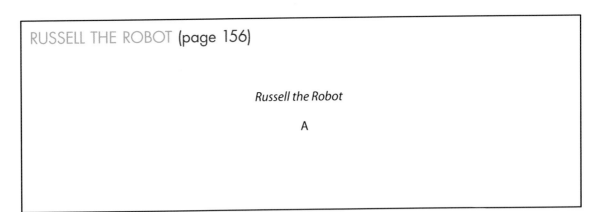

Russell the Robot

A

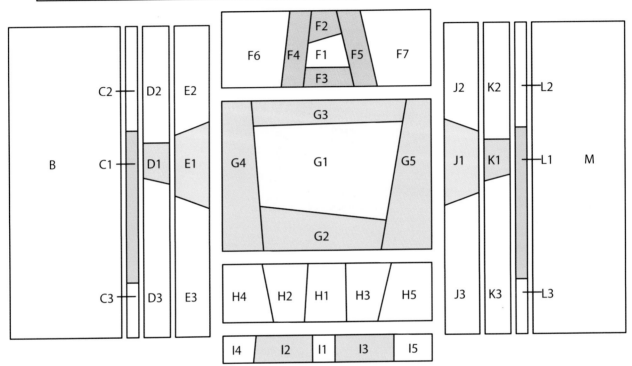

B

C2 · D2 · E2

C1 · D1 · E1

C3 · D3 · E3

F6 · F4 · F2 · F1 · F5 · F7
F3

G3
G4 · G1 · G5
G2

J2 · K2 · L2

J1 · K1 · L1

J3 · K3 · L3

M

H4 · H2 · H1 · H3 · H5

I4 · I2 · I1 · I3 · I5

N

Enlarge 200% and add ¼″ seam allowance to all sides.

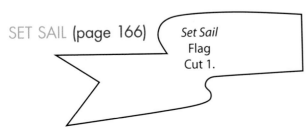

Set Sail
Flag
Cut 1.

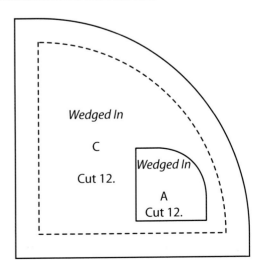

Wedged In

C

Cut 12.

Wedged In

A
Cut 12.

SLOT MACHINE (page 172)

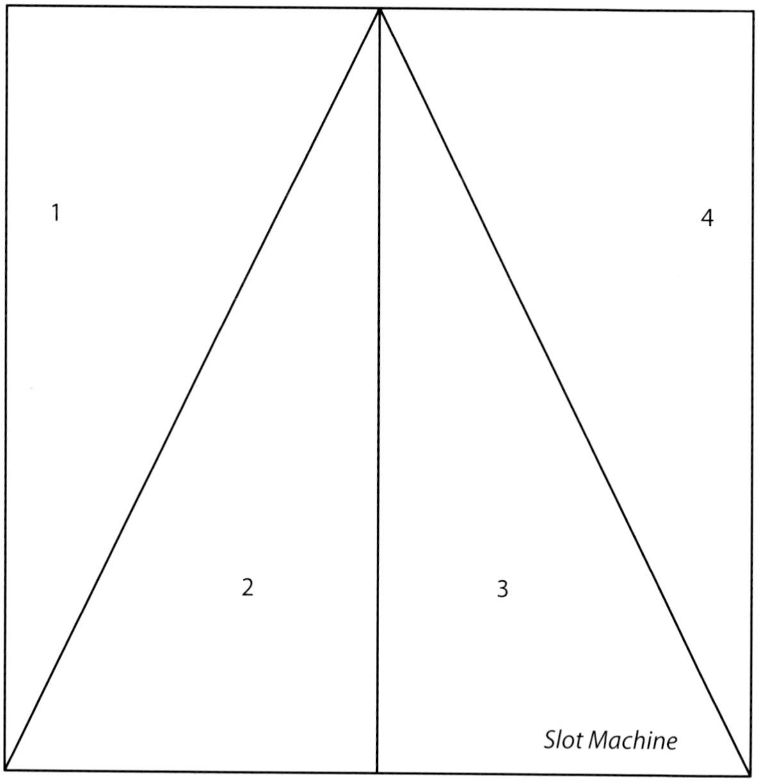

1

4

2

3

Slot Machine

Add ¼″ seam allowances to all sides.

PINWHEEL (page 138)

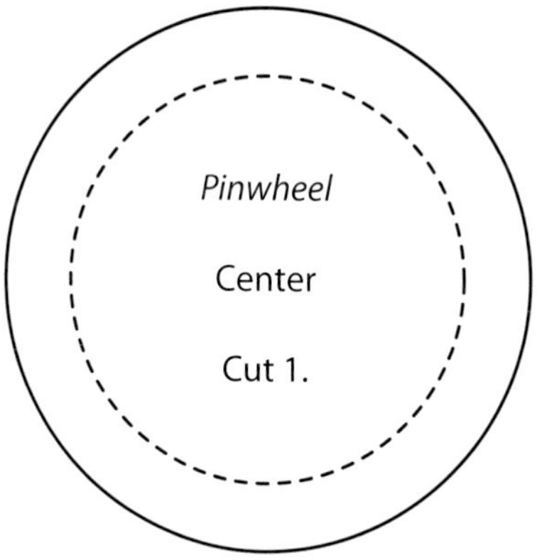

Pinwheel

Center

Cut 1.

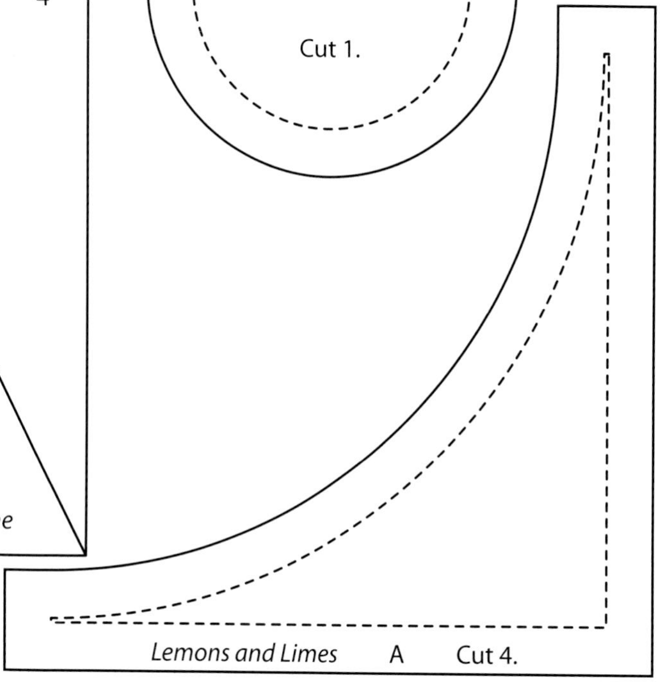

Lemons and Limes   A   Cut 4.

LEMONS AND LIMES (page 102)

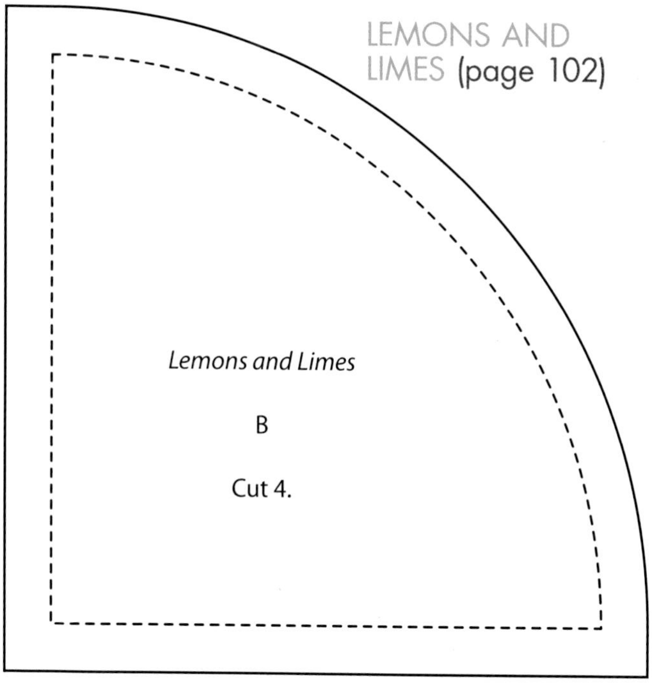

Lemons and Limes

B

Cut 4.

WEDGED IN (page 196)

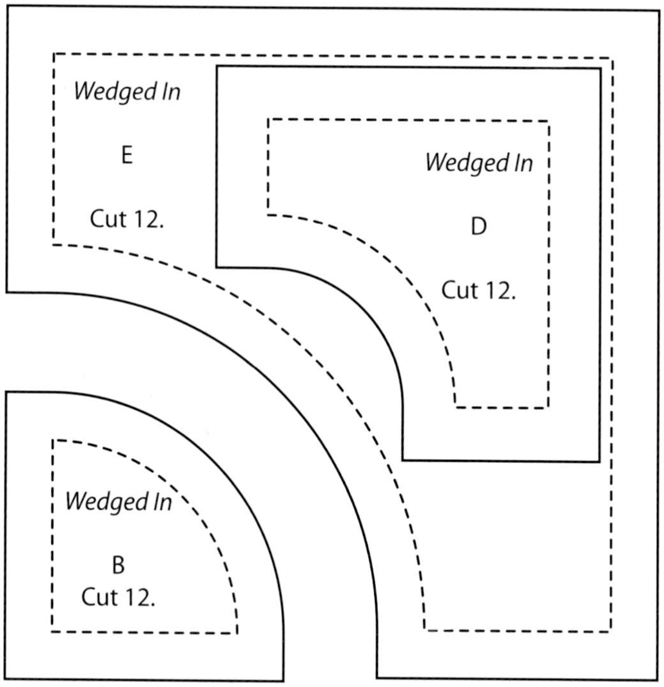

Wedged In

E

Cut 12.

Wedged In

D

Cut 12.

Wedged In

B
Cut 12.

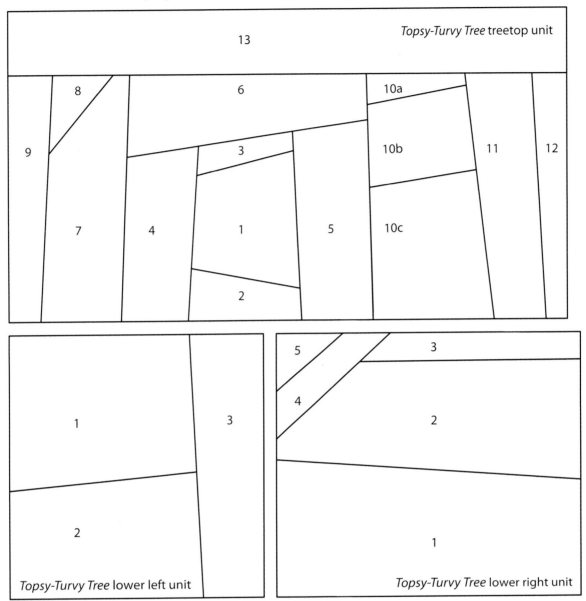

Topsy-Turvy Tree treetop unit

Topsy-Turvy Tree lower left unit

Topsy-Turvy Tree lower right unit

Enlarge 200% and add ¼″ seam allowances to all sides.

Topsy-Turvy Tree

WINDMILL (page 198)

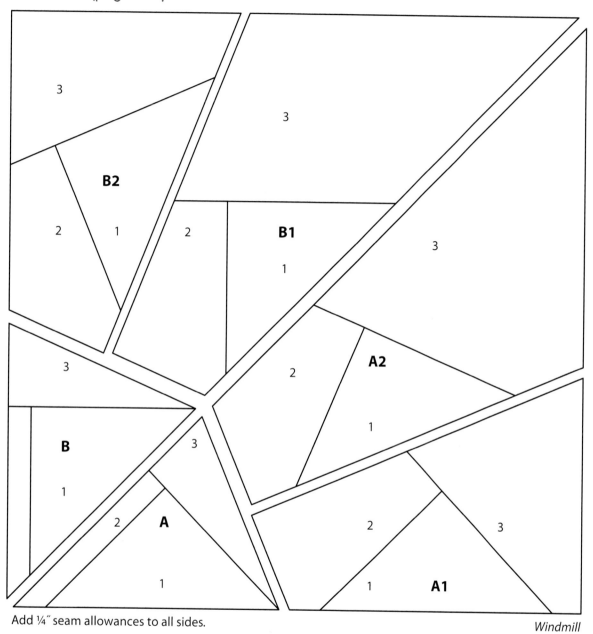

Add ¼″ seam allowances to all sides.

Windmill

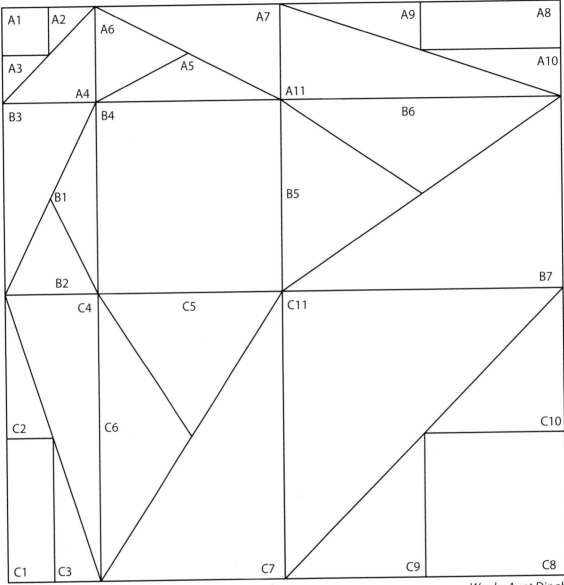

Enlarge 200% and add ¼″ seam allowances to each piece.

Wonky Aunt Dinah

DESIGNERS

Bari J. Ackerman	barij.typepad.com	Faith Jones	freshlemonsquilts.com
John Q. Adams	quiltdad.com	Nicole Kaplan	patchworkduck.com
Cheryl Arkison	naptimequilter.blogspot.com	Susan Brubaker Knapp	bluemoonriver.com
Ellen Luckett Baker	thelongthread.com	Wayne Kollinger	tuxedoparkdesign.com
Alethea Ballard	maverickquilts.com	Laura West Kong	laurawestkong.com
Briana Arlene Balsam	briana-arlene.blogspot.com	Penny Michelle Layman	sewtakeahike.typepad.com
Mo Beldell	limegardenias.blogspot.com	Yvonne Malone	yvonnemalonestudio.com
Natalia Bonner	piecenquilt.com	Sherri McConnell	aquiltinglife.com
Heather Bostic	alamodefabric.blogspot.com	Jamie Moilanen	flickr.com/photos/30737301@N05
Jessica Brown	justgiveitago.blogspot.com	Louise Papas	lululollylegs.blogspot.com
Natasha Bruecher	haniesquilts.blogspot.com	Angela Pingel	cuttopieces.blogspot.com
Sonja Callaghan	artisania.wordpress.com	Weeks Ringle and Bill Kerr	funquilts.com
Emily Cier	carolinapatchworks.com/blog	Rachel Roxburgh	roxycreations.blogspot.com
Leanne Cohen	quiltsabit.blogspot.com	Latifah Saafir	thequiltengineer.com
Melissa Crow	checkoutgirlcrafts.blogspot.com	Amanda Sasikirana	amandasasikirana.wordpress.com
Monique Dillard	opengatequilts.com	Kim Schaefer	littlequiltcompany.com
Kirsten Duncan	pompomrouge.com	Elizabeth Scott	latebloomerquilts.com
Amy Ellis	amyscreativeside.blogspot.com	Amy Sinibaldi	nanacompany.typepad.com
Lara Finlayson	thornberry.wordpress.com	Pat Sloan	patsloan.com
Krista Fleckenstein	spottedstone.blogspot.com	Tiffany Stephens	lcmquilt.com
Lynne Goldsworthy	lilysquilts.blogspot.com	Kirsti Underwood	stitchystitcherson.blogspot.com
Ann Haley	sportsew.wordpress.com	Kimberly Walus	bittybitsandpieces.blogspot.com
Natalie Hardin	schoolofcrafts.blogspot.com	Monika Wintermantel	monaw.blogspot.com
Kate Henderson	neverenoughhours.blogspot.com	Susanne Woods	beyondthekids.com
Krista Hennebury	poppyprintcreates.blogspot.com	Vivianne (Viv) Wride	sewvivid.com
Wendy Hill	wendyhill.net/blog	Angela Yosten	angelayosten.com
Solidia Hubbard	modernsewl.blogspot.com		

stashBOOKS®

fabric arts for a handmade lifestyle

If you're craving beautiful authenticity in a time of mass-production...Stash Books is for you. Stash Books is a line of how-to books celebrating fabric arts for a handmade lifestyle. Backed by C&T Publishing's solid reputation for quality, Stash Books will inspire you with contemporary designs, clear and simple instructions, and engaging photography.

www.stashbooks.com